How to Decipher the Menu
Know the Market Foods
&
Embark on a Tasting Adventure

Carol L. Schroeder and Katrina A. Schroeder

GINKGO PRESS INC

Madison, Wisconsin

Eat Smart in Denmark
Carol L. Schroeder and Katrina A. Schroeder

The quote by James A. Michener from "This Great Big Wonderful World," from the March 1956 issue of Travel-Holiday Magazine, © 1956 by James A. Michener, is reprinted by permission of William Morris Endeavor Entertainment on behalf of the publisher.

Publisher's Cataloging-in-Publication
(*Provided by Quality Books, Inc.*)
Schroeder, Carol. L.
   Eat smart in Denmark : how to decipher the menu, know
the market foods & embark on a tasting adventure / Carol
L. Schroeder, Katrina A. Schroeder.
   Includes bibliographical references and index.
   LCCN 2014933690
   ISBN 978-1-938489-02-0

   1. Cooking, Danish. 2. Diet--Denmark. 3. Food
habits--Denmark. 4. Cooking--Denmark. 5. Denmark--
Guidebooks. I. Schroeder, Katrina A. II. Title.

TX722.D4S37 2014   641.59481
                  QBI14-600044

Printed in the United States of America

In memory of

Kate Bengtsen and Niels Ingwersen

who inspired our love of Denmark

Æret være deres minde

Contents

Preface   ix
Acknowledgments   xi

The Cuisine of Denmark   1
An historical survey of the development of Danish cuisine.

    The Earliest Inhabitants   1
    Birth of Agriculture during the Neolithic Period   2
    Denmark during the Bronze and Iron Ages   3
    The Viking Era   4
    The Kalmar Union: Denmark as a Super Power   7
    Life under the Absolute Monarchy   9
    Agricultural Reform in the Late 19th Century   11
    Denmark in Recent Times   13
    A Revitalization of Danish Cuisine   16

Regional Danish Food   19
A quick tour of Danish foods and their regional variations.

    Danish Food in a Nutshell   19
    The Regions of Denmark   26
      The Island of Zealand   27
      The Island of Funen   29
      The Jutland Peninsula   30
      The Island of Bornholm   34
    Danish Holiday Traditions   35

Tastes of Denmark   43
A selection of delicious, authentic recipes to try before leaving home. Many are easy to prepare.

Shopping in Denmark's Food Markets   69
Tips to increase your savvy in outdoor and indoor food markets, specialty shops, and in purchasing street foods.

Resources   71

Stores that sell hard-to-find Danish foods, some Danish bakeries and restaurants in North America, online social networking, news, tour and travel information.

Suppliers of Danish Food Items   71
Online, News, and Social Information   75
Tours, Travel Advice, and Useful Organizations   76

Helpful Phrases   79

Phrases in English translated to Danish, with additional phonetic interpretation, which will assist you in finding, ordering, and buying foods or ingredients.

In the Restaurant   79
In the Market   81
Other Useful Phrases   82

Menu Guide   83

An extensive listing of menu entries in Danish, with English translations, to make ordering food an easy and immediately rewarding experience.

Foods and Flavors Guide   107

A comprehensive glossary of ingredients, kitchen utensils, and cooking methods in Danish, with English translations.

Food Establishments   135

A quick reference guide to restaurants visited.

Bibliography   137
Index   139

Preface

> If you reject the food, ignore the customs, fear the
> religion and avoid the people, you might better
> stay home. You are like a pebble thrown into
> water; you become wet on the surface but you are
> never a part of the water.
>
> —JAMES A. MICHENER

Denmark is probably the only country in the world where asking visitors to pronounce the name of a popular dessert has reached the level of a national sport. One of my claims to expertise in Danish culture, aside from my master's degree in Scandinavian Studies, is the fact that none other than the famed Danish comedian Victor Borge once laughed at my pronunciation of *rødgrød med fløde*—and I can say it better than most foreigners.

My interest in Danish culture dates back to a fateful day in high school, in a small town in New Jersey, when I passed a note to a new girl. Annette turned out to be a young Dane on a private exchange-student arrangement. Impressed by the fact that her official Danish Scout uniform included both a Smokey the Bear hat and a buckle that could be used as a bottle opener, my friends and I invited her to become a member of our Girl Scout troop. That initial encounter led me to visit Annette in Denmark when I was 16, which was my first introduction to the delights of Danish cuisine.

At that time Danish food had not changed much for several decades, and emphasized bread and cheese for breakfast, open-faced sandwiches (*smørrebrød*) for lunch, and meat (especially pork) or fish with potatoes for dinner. In between, of course, came those delicious Danish pastries. Who wouldn't love a country where mid-morning coffee, mid-afternoon tea, and after-dinner coffee were often accompanied by something sweet? My fate was decided, and I went on to spend a year at the University of Copenhagen before getting a master's degree in Scandinavian Studies at the University of Wisconsin. My husband Dean and I then opened a retail store, Orange Tree Imports, which is strongly influenced by Scandinavian design.

Our son and daughter became regular visitors to Denmark starting at an early age, and I like to think that Katrina's early exposure to Danish cuisine helped spark her interest in food, leading her to pursue a career as a Registered Dietitian. She shares my love of traditional Danish food, and it has been a delight having her as my co-author on this exploration of the cuisine in Denmark.

Today's Danish culinary scene is much more international in scope than it was when I first visited in 1969. There is also a very active local foods movement in Denmark (and all of Scandinavia) that focuses on making use of regional ingredients, especially seafood and produce, to create variations on traditional food and drink. The Copenhagen restaurant Noma has been voted number one for four times in the World's 50 Best Restaurant Awards sponsored by S. Pellegrino. Noma stands for *Nordic Mad* (which means "Nordic food"), a tribute to its regional approach to food and its leadership role in this New Nordic Cuisine Movement.

The average visitor to Denmark is not likely to eat at Noma—there is a three-month wait for reservations, and radishes in edible dirt are not to everyone's taste—but there are hundreds of places in Denmark to eat both traditional and "New Nordic" foods. It is our hope that this book will help guide you through the world of Danish food. There are five main sections: an encapsulated history of Danish cuisine, an overview of contemporary cuisine including regional and seasonal specialties, and then recipes adapted for the American kitchen. These are followed by two Danish/English glossaries, one listing dishes you might find on a Danish menu (complete with recommendations), and the other listing food items and terms associated with the preparing and serving of food.

To make your exploration of Danish cuisine easier, we also include a section of helpful phrases, information about shopping in a Danish market, resources for finding ingredients in the US, and a bibliography of books in English about Danish food. Enjoy!

CAROL SCHROEDER & KATRINA SCHROEDER
Madison, Wisconsin

Acknowledgments

Many individuals and organizations both in Denmark and North America generously shared their time and expertise with us as we worked on *Eat Smart in Denmark*. Our first thanks must go to Joan Peterson, who created the EAT SMART series and gave us the opportunity to write this book exploring the cuisine of one of our favorite countries. We encourage you to look at the other guides in this series, many of them written by Joan herself.

Our Danish friends Annette and Søren Jessen, Trilby Gustafson, and Grethe Jacobsen hosted our very enjoyable research trip to Denmark, and Grethe and her husband Jens Christian Johansen have patiently answered countless food questions since our return. Annette and Søren went over page after page of culinary terms while traveling with us in Canada, gamely finishing the last few as we waited in an emergency room in Calgary after Søren was struck with appendicitis.

On the first day of our trip to learn more about Danish food, Lykke Pedersen of The National Museum of Denmark guided us through the museum's extensive cultural exhibitions and also treated us to lunch in the employee cafeteria, where we learned that historians eat quite well in Denmark. The next day Ellen Dahl led us on a behind-the-scenes tour of Tivoli, including interviews with several chefs. And thanks to Grethe Jacobsen, we had the honor of visiting food historian Bi Skaarup on her farm Elysium in Nordfalster. Restaurant expert Bent Christensen gave us the opportunity to meet many well-known Scandinavian chefs at the launch party for his latest book about the best Nordic restaurants.

We are very grateful to all those who granted us interviews and contributed recipes (some of which could not be used due to space limitations). They included Chef Frederik Hvidt of Marv og Ben, Chef Kasper Kallerup Hansen of Hotel Orø Kro, Den Skaldede Kok Carsten Olsen, restauranteur Poul

Eriksen of Grøften, Den Røde Cottage chef Anita Klemensen, Chef Martin Bjørn of Brdr. Price in Tivoli, Chef Thorleif Aagaard of Søstrene Olsen, Sortebro Krø chef John Kofod Petersen, Restaurant Carlslund chef Henning Engstrøm, Norsminde Kro chef Søren Pedersen, Malling og Schmidt chef Thorston Schmidt, Restaurant Els chef David Loehr, Conditori La Glace owner Marianne Stagetorn Kolos, and Gammel Mønt chef Claus Christensen. Camilla Plum, author of *The Scandinavian Kitchen*, and Kevin Crafts, author of *Ebelskivers*, gave us permission to use recipes from their books.

In the US we received help every step of the way from the members of Carol's Danish book club, including Inge Bentzen, Anne Marie Correll, Stephanie Fassnacht, Anne Birgitte Gebauer, Anette Hansen, Faith Ingwersen, Palle Pedersen, and Solveig Rossi. Nete Schmidt and Kirsten Wolf of the University of Wisconsin–Madison Scandinavian Studies Department patiently answered our questions, and Kirsten also proofread the manuscript, enthusiastically offering many excellent suggestions.

We strongly believe that recipes should be tested after they've been translated into English (and American measurements). A team of cooks around the country generously helped us with this task, often sending back comments and even photos. Many thanks to our recipe testers: Kirsten Berg-Sonne, Marianne Busse, Sarah Marie Christiansen, Edward Chwae, Anne Churchill, Jenni Collins, Anniken Davenport, Chantelle Driever, Susie Feest, Anna Hoover, Emily Kelly, Gloria Lawrence, Mary Kay Madsen, Lynn McCarty, Sara O'Shea, Regan Quick-Severin, Dean Schroeder, Alex Smith, Judy Tanenbaum, Sheila Tow, and Jan Vidruk. Tim Brooks was also a great help in answering our many fish questions.

Several experts have reviewed sections of the chapters about Danish food history and regional specialty for accuracy: Søren Riisgaard Mortensen; Bjarne Clement of the Ribe VikingeCenter; Ole Troelsø, author of *The Insider's Guide to Smørrebrød*; Helle Mogensen of Destination Bornholm and Poul-Erik Transø on the cuisine of Bornholm; Inger Heldbjerg Busk of the Odense City Museums; and Inge Adriansen of Museum Sønderjylland.

Thanks also to the University of Wisconsin Press, Ole Troelsø, Jason Ilstrup of HotelRED in Madison, and Sanne Ytting of The Copenhagen in New York for their enthusiastic help in promoting our project.

We owe a great debt of gratitude to the editorial team at Ginkgo Press for their encouragement, guidance, and hard work on this project. Without Joan Peterson, Susan Chwae, and Brook Soltvedt, *Eat Smart in Denmark* would not have become a reality.

Photo credits
Photos by Carol and Katrina Schroeder unless otherwise noted.

On the front cover:
Claus Christensen, Restaurant Gammel Mønt
Svogerslev Kro—photo courtesy of Kim Frost
Smørrebrød—photo by Maie Hatcher

On the back cover:
Norsminde Kro, Odder, Jutland
Othello Cake at Conditori La Glace
Schønnemannschnaps Specialty—photo courtesy of Restaurant Schønnemann
Henrik Walbom, head waiter at Restaurant Lumskebugten, serving
    smoked salmon and potato *smørrebrød*—*Insider's Guide to Smørrebrød*
    by Ole Troelsø
Øllebrød med Æggesnaps—My Danish Kitchen blog by Gitte Gentile
Authors—photo by Alex Smith

Special thanks for help sourcing the black-and-white photos:
Danish Dairy Board: Eva Højmark
Odense City Museums: Inger Heldbjerg Busk
Aalborg Aquavit & Patchwork Group: Jacob H. Scriver
Røgeriet Svaneke: Ricko
Tulip Food Company: Rune Jungberg Pedersen

Special thanks for help sourcing the color photos:
Page One:
Ribe VikingeCenter—Diana Berthelsen
Silkeborg Kulturhistoriske Museum—Ole Nielsen

Page Two:
Den Gamle By—Merete Pallesen
Vaniljekranse—My Danish Kitchen blog by Gitte Gentile

Page Three:
Æbleskiver—RICE Denmark: Dagmar Top Haustrup
Rødgrød—photo by Emilie Zenia Andersen
Kransekage—Odense Marcipan: Morten Rosenberg

ACKNOWLEDGMENTS

Pastries—Lauras Bakery: Kristian Vangsgaard
Sønderjysk Coffee Table—Museum Sønderjylland: Inge Adriansen

Page Four:
Leverpostej and *Sol over Gudhjem*—The Danish Sandwich blog by
   Marcus Schioler
Smørrebrød platters—Restaurant Kronborg: Walther Griesé; photo by
   Chris Tonnesen

Page Five:
Smushi—The Royal Café, Copenhagen
Ida Davidsen Restaurant—Oscar Davidsen Siesbye
Riberhus Esrom *smørrebrød*—Arla Foods: Marianne Kristensen, Rikke
   Halberg Mandsholm, and Astrid Gade Nielsen

Page Six:
Flæskesteg—Danish Agriculture and Food Council: Birgit Mulbjerg

Page Seven:
Noma dish—Photo from *Culinaire Saisonnier*
Claus Meyer—Meyers ApS: Peter Warberg

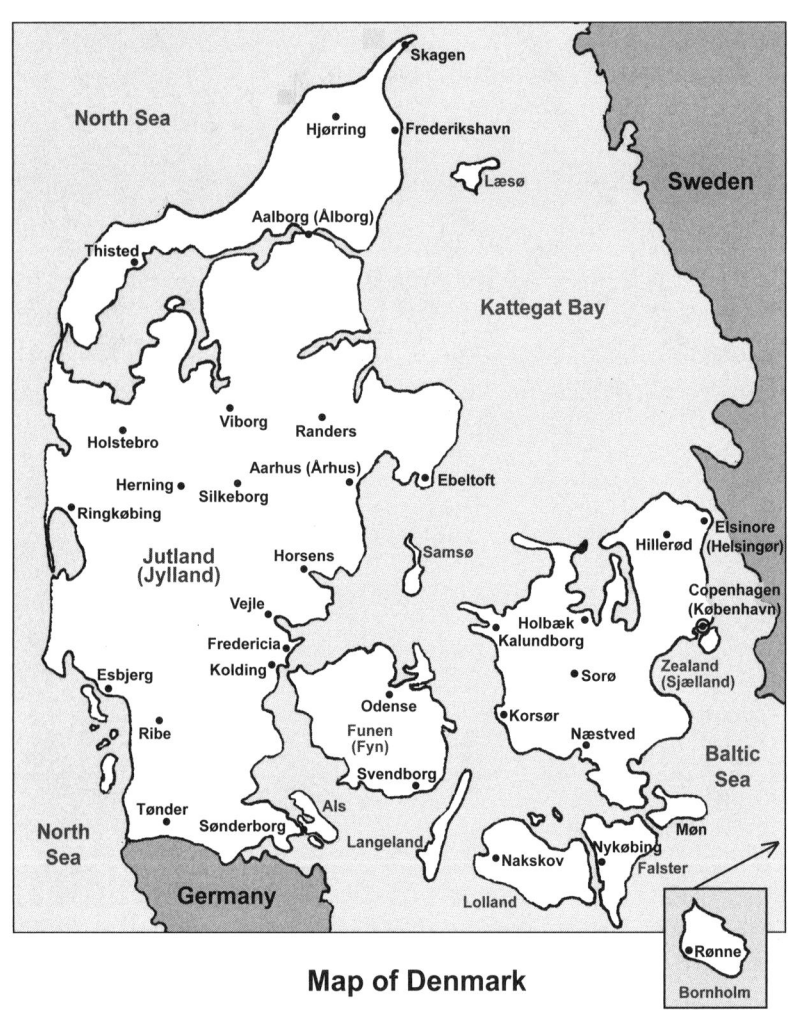

Map of Denmark

The Cuisine of Denmark

An Historical Survey

Denmark's climate is not as harsh as that of its Scandinavian neighbors. The Gulf Stream keeps the weather surprisingly warm, considering that Copenhagen is at the same latitude as Juneau, Alaska. However winters are long and dark, with only seven hours of light between sunrise and sunset on the shortest day of the year. The growing season is also relatively short, although daylight in the summer months may last for eighteen hours. Proximity to the sea throughout Denmark has always provided good access to seafood, and fresh and smoked fish have been staples of the Danish diet through the ages. Hunting and eventually the domestication of animals put meat on the table, and foraging followed by agricultural cultivation added a limited array of vegetables, fruits, and potatoes in season. Preservation by drying, smoking, cheesemaking, and fermentation allowed foods to be stored for consumption during the remainder of the year. These ancient methods of food preservation are undergoing a renaissance as part of the New Nordic Cuisine movement.

The Earliest Inhabitants

Danes today enjoy a wide variety of foodstuffs, and Denmark exports meat and dairy products—especially cheese, bacon, and butter—around the world. But the first prehistoric residents of what we now know as Denmark had very few food options. These earliest inhabitants can be traced back to the end of the last ice age, which was the beginning of the long period of time referred to as the Stone Age. The familiar concept of naming these early historical eras based on the use of tools made of different materials—the Stone Age, Iron Age, and Bronze Age—originated in Denmark with archeologist Christian Jürgensen Thomsen in 1825.

The Stone Age can be divided into three parts: the Paleolithic period (to 12,500 BCE), the Mesolithic period (12,500 to 3900 BCE), and the Neolithic period (3900 to 1700 BCE). As the climate warmed and the glaciers of the ice age receded, it became possible for Paleolithic nomadic hunters to migrate into the tundra-covered land that is now Denmark. There they lived mostly on reindeer, but over the next millennium, as the dense primeval forest developed, hunters were able to kill other wild game, including red deer, roe deer, and wild boars. However, in contrast to the current preconception about the totally protein-based "paleo" diet, excavations show that the inhabitants of Denmark during this period also ate carbohydrates in the form of foraged roots, acorns, seeds, and grasses.

In the early Mesolithic period the sea level rose, drowning the land that had once connected Denmark with what is now Britain and Sweden. The rising water also divided much of northern Denmark into islands, creating new fjords and increasing the miles of coast and shoreline. In addition to hunting game, some groups established seasonal fishing stations to procure seafood and marine animals such as seals. Fishing nets, leisters (spears with barbed prongs), and weirs (traps) were eventually developed to catch fish. The quantities of oyster and mussel shells found in excavated domestic rubbish heaps called *køkkenmøddinger* (kitchen middens), dated to between 5100 and 4100 BCE, testify to the importance of this new abundance of shellfish in the late Stone Age diet in some areas.

The Birth of Agriculture during the Neolithic Period

Starting in about 3900 BCE, during the Neolithic period of the Stone Age, there is early evidence of agriculture in Denmark. Neolithic people traveled great distances in the dugout canoes that first came into use in Mesolithic times. It was through contact with the south that the Neolithic Danes learned about growing crops, animal husbandry, and the production of pottery for cooking and serving vessels. These early travelers brought grains and possibly even domesticated animals home with them from as far away as the Middle East. Forests were cleared by burning and later by the use of sharpened flint axes, and small communities began to be formed by these previously migrant people. This made food production possible, and cattle, pigs, and sheep were kept as domesticated animals to supplement the food obtained by hunting and fishing. Thousands of dolmens and passage graves called *gravhøje* (burial mounds) from this period still dot the Danish landscape.

Denmark during the Bronze and Iron Ages

The Bronze Age (1700 to 500 BCE) marked the real start of farming as more land was put to use for cultivation and grazing, increasing year-round food options. Late Bronze Age burials revealed sophisticated weapons, shields, and the bronze *lurs* (*lurer* horns) that are famous as the trademark of Danish Lurpak butter today. Because Denmark produced neither copper nor tin, it was contact with people in other areas such as the southern parts of Central Europe that allowed Danes to create objects out of bronze, including these tools and weapons. Many archeological finds from this period, including an artistic ritual artifact depicting a horse-drawn carriage carrying the sun disk, found in a bog in Zealand, are considered to be among the most valuable treasures on display in Copenhagen at the National Museum of Denmark.

The Iron Age (500 BCE to 800 AD) is so named because the use of iron for making tools and weapons allowed the Danes to exploit their own deposits of bog iron ore, creating tools and weapons of forged iron that were stronger and lighter than cast bronze. The Roman Empire was flourishing to the south during the latter part of this period (known as the Roman Iron Age), and access to Roman trade introduced goods such as drinking glasses, bronze bowls, and gold and silver items to the Danish culture.

Danes today can revisit their Stone Age and Iron Age roots in the Sagnlandet Lejre, or Land of Legends Centre for Historical-Archaeological Research and Communication, in Lejre near Roskilde on the island of Zealand. This open-air park, founded in 1964 by ethnologist Hans-Ole

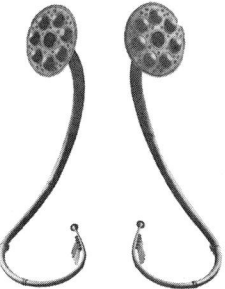 

Lurs were blown in pairs during religious ceremonies during the Bronze Age. The Danish company Lurmark registered their logo featuring these *lurs* in 1901 as the trademark for quality Danish butter. Butter image courtesy of the Danish Agriculture & Food Council.

Hansen, includes a Stone Age campsite from 5000 BCE as well as an Iron Age village and sacrificial bog dating from 200 BCE to 200 AD.

Families and school groups can spend time in the part of Lejre known as Lethra living as though in the Iron Age. Those who become part of this living history exhibit are provided with basic food ingredients such as grains, milk and cream, meat, beans, apples, nuts, onions, and mushrooms. They are also encouraged to gather wild fruits and plants or other species within the Lejre historic compound to complement their meals.

Research, including that conducted in Lejre, has shown that Iron Age Danes used a rudimentary scratch-plow called an ard to grow flax, barley, emmer, and einkorn wheat. They harvested these grains in the fall using a sickle, then threshed the grain, crushed it into flour, kneaded it into bread, or used it to make porridge.

These early Danes kept some livestock, and in the winter the domesticated animals—which included cattle, sheep, and pigs—shared the house with the people. This arrangement helped provide warmth during the long, cold months. Some animals were kept primarily for their milk, which was used right away or made into cheese. Cuts of meat (both domestic and hunted) were preserved by suspending them from the rafters of the houses to cure in the smoke from the hearth fire, often fueled with peat from the bogs. When available, wild berries, apples, and nuts supplemented the diet, and seafood continued to be a staple.

Meats were cooked on spits over the fireplace in the house, and bread was baked in the ashes of the hearth fire. Earthenware vessels were used for cooking dishes such as porridge or gruel. Studies of the incredibly well-preserved remains of the Tollund Man (300 to 400 BCE), found in a peat bog near Silkeborg in Jutland in 1950, show that his last meal was a mixture of barley, rye, and oats. Other bog finds also show only grains in the digestive system, indicating that meat was perhaps a rare feature in the diet of the time. The Tollund Man, together with an exhibition about the Iron Age in Denmark, can be seen today in the Silkeborg Museum.

The Viking Era

In about 700 AD, Denmark began to become a unified entity, in part to defend itself against invasions from the south. This new centralized nation became recognized as a world power when Vikings brutally destroyed the Lindisfarne Abbey off the coast of northeast England in 793. For the next 300 years, ending with the Battle of Hastings in 1066, the Vikings were a force to be reckoned with throughout Europe and even into Russia. Key events of this time include the peaceful introduction of Christianity to Denmark under political pressure during the second half of the 10th century, and England being under Danish rule from 1015 to 1042.

The food of the Vikings was not dramatically different from that of the Iron Age, although there was more widespread agriculture and animal husbandry. Grains such as rye, barley, and wheat were made into bread or porridge, and meat (often venison or pork) was boiled into a stew. Turnips, beans, peas, and white carrots were cultivated and could be added when in season. Seafood such as herring, cod, and shellfish were also staples of the Viking diet. There is evidence that two meals a day were the norm, a "day meal" eaten two hours after starting work, and a "night meal" eaten in the evening.

Preservation of food for the long winters and for sea voyages was a constant concern. In addition to smoking or salting fish and meat, the Vikings became skilled in fermentation, sausage making, and pickling. They also dried vegetables, and preserved cow, goat, and sheep milk by making butter and cheese. In about 1000 AD the Vikings developed a method to make cheese by pressing and salting curdled milk, and two centuries later a document was issued (Kong Valdemars Jordebog, 1231) that mentions cheese being used to pay taxes to the king and church. Vikings also drank fresh milk when it was available.

Their drinks of choice, however, were beer or ale brewed from barley, and mead made from fermented honey and water. Even children drank the weak, sweet beer daily, in part because water in the more urban areas could be polluted and water used for brewing was made safe by boiling. Another popular Viking Age drink was *bjorr*, a strong liquor made from fermented apple or pear cider. The Vikings often served these fermented drinks in a cauldron, and guests helped themselves with wooden or pottery bowls. (The popular contemporary drinking toast "*Skål!*" stems from this period, and literally means "Bowl!") The polished hollow drinking horns we associate with this period were probably reserved for ceremonial occasions.

The Vikings kept domesticated livestock such as cattle, horses, sheep, pigs, goats, and hens to supplement their fishing and their hunting of game and wild birds. Meat was usually eaten boiled, using a large iron, clay, or soapstone pot, either placed directly on the fire or hung above it on iron chains. Iron hooks would be used to pull the pieces of meat or fish out of the boiling liquid, to which vegetables and other ingredients could be added.

Viking drinking horns like the reproductions from the Ribe VikingeCenter shown on the left have inspired drinking vessels ranging from elaborate late-medieval ceremonial horns gilded with bronze (center) to the ceramic beer stein on the right, produced by Tuborg the 1960s. Medieval drinking horn image courtesy of the University of Wisconsin–Madison Memorial Library Department of Special Collections.

Fire-heated stones about the size of a hand were sometimes used to speed up the cooking process. These were taken out of the ashes and put into the liquid until they cooled, at which time they were put back into the fire again. After several uses these cooking stones began to break up and had to be disposed of. An abundance of fire-exposed stones have been found in archeological excavations of Viking homes.

Other Viking cooking equipment included hooks and spits for roasting, and ovens for baking. Frying pans and warming griddles have also been discovered in archeological digs. Forks were used in cooking, especially to retrieve pieces of meat from the liquid in the kettle. Spoons and ladles made of wood or bone (some of which had flatter bowls than modern spoons) were common utensils, as were knives made of iron.

The cereal crops grown by the Vikings included oats, rye, barley, and wheat, but rye was the most common grain. Rye bread, which is a staple in today's Danish cuisine, may date back over 1,500 years in Denmark. Burned grains and straw found in early ovens for melting iron ore have been found to be from rye and barley, making rye cultivation older than previously thought—perhaps starting as early as 200 to 300 AD. Rye is particularly well suited to the Danish climate, and even today the average Dane eats about 45–50 pounds of *rugbrød* (rye bread) per year. Rye was introduced to the British by the Vikings, who hand-milled their flour on round grindstones often made of lava stone imported from the Rhineland.

Most bread was unleavened and was baked over the fire on flat iron or stone plates that produced a thick, pancake-style bread. However the Vikings also made some raised breads using wild yeasts, raising agents such as buttermilk and sour milk, and leftover yeast from brewing. They also used the sourdough method, creating a starter by allowing flour and water to stand several days to ferment.

Today's Danish cuisine features remnants of its Viking ancestry in dishes using smoked pork, dried cod, salt-cured salmon, and pickled herring, as well as the unique rye bread and beer porridge known as *øllebrød*. Thanks to the work of the late historian Bi Skaarup and the local restaurant Snekken, visitors to the Viking Ship Museum in Roskilde can dine in the Café Knarr on "New Nordic Viking Food" made with ingredients used during the Viking Age. Specialty dishes include flat bread, dried smoked fish, sausages, beer, grains, and meat wrapped in seaweed, sorrel, or other local leafy plants. Viking cooking and bread-baking can be experienced at the Ribe VikingeCenter, a living museum that recreates three different Viking environments: the Market Place and an adjoining ship from the early 8th century; the Great Farm from 980 AD, which includes a longhouse with five connected buildings; and eight town houses from the year 825 AD.

The Kalmar Union: Denmark as a Superpower

The Danish diet during the Middle Ages (about 1050 to 1550) relied heavily on grains, especially barley and rye, as well as seafood and some meat. It was during this time that the custom of marinating herring became a popular way to preserve the fish, and even today marinated herring is a staple of traditional Danish cuisine.

It is King Erik V (1249 to 1286) whom we have to thank for the wonderful system of inns in Denmark. He decreed that there should be stage posts for his men at regular intervals throughout the land. The inn, or *kro*, became a Danish institution, and many of these inns with their half-timbered walls and thatched roofs still stand today. A few continue to provide accommodations, and many offer a traditional menu of what is known as *kromad*, or inn food.

Denmark was, with interruptions, one of the major European powers between the 13th and 17th centuries. Under the rule of Margrete I of Denmark (1353 to 1412) the kingdom spanned over a million square miles, compared to the 16,600 square miles that make up Denmark today (if one does not include Greenland or the Faroe Islands). The Kalmar Union was a series of agreements from 1397 to 1523 that united Norway (which then included Iceland, Greenland, Shetland, and the Orkney Islands) and Sweden (which then included Finland) under the Danish monarchy.

Sortebro Kro is a traditional Danish inn on the island Funen. The inn, which dates from 1805, was moved from its original location and rebuilt as a working restaurant in the living history museum called The Funen Village in Odense. Courtesy of the Odense City Museums.

In 1523 Sweden broke out of the union and became an independent kingdom, rising to become a major European power during the following two centuries. Conflicts between Sweden and Denmark were to prove costly for both countries, with eleven Dano-Swedish wars between 1521 and 1814.

Denmark became Protestant in 1536, and the period known as the Renaissance is usually considered to span from the date of the Reformation until the establishment of the absolute monarchy in 1660. A popular contemporary dish that dates back to this period is *frikadeller*, meatballs, which are today made of ground pork and veal sautéed in butter (see recipe, p. 48). At that time they were made of pure pork, and would most likely have been a dish for the upper classes. In the Middle Ages meat was a rarity for peasants, who subsisted mostly on grains and fish.

Rural families supplemented these staples by growing their own vegetables, including kale, on the common farmlands. Kale has long been an important source of vitamin C throughout Scandinavia in the winter months, and in fact the original Danish word for a garden was *kålgård* (kale garden).

This peasant vegetable was, however, not considered refined enough for the upper-class palate. In 1520, King Christian II brought a large group of Dutch families to the island of Amager, just outside Copenhagen's city gates, to have them grow produce for the royal household. Dutch agriculture was more advanced than that of Denmark at the time, and these farmers were responsible for the growing—and lasting—popularity of cabbage in the Danish diet, and for the introduction of the carrot to Danish agriculture.

In 1521 we find the earliest known reference in Denmark to what is now known as *akvavit* (aquavit, literally, "water of life"). *Akvavit* is a distilled spirit made from either grain or potatoes and flavored with spices such as caraway and dill. Originally thought to have medicinal powers, *akvavit*—also known as *snaps*—is still a part of traditional celebrations and is often served with the first course at formal lunches. A popular toast when drinking *snaps* is *"Skål!"* (the Danish equivalent of "Cheers!"), which comes from the Old Norse word for a bowl—the Viking drinking vessel of choice.

Coffee has been a national drink in Denmark almost since its introduction in the 1660s, although its popularity initially was limited to noblewomen. Danes today drink almost 20 pounds of coffee per person each year, ranking them number 4 in the world in coffee consumption.

Life under the Absolute Monarchy

A coup by King Frederik III established absolute monarchy in Denmark in 1660, and this endured until 1848 when there was a peaceful revolution following the death of Christian VIII. (All Danish kings after 1513 are conveniently named either Frederik or Christian.) The monarch had considerable power, together with the clergy, and there was a great difference between the lives of the rural farming class, the rising tradesman class living in market towns, and the upper class residing in the great manor houses and castles.

Denmark's nobility brought cooks from France who made soups, fancy pastries, white bread, and cream sauces such as the béchamel sauce that is today used in *stegt flæsk og persillesovs* (slices of fried pork belly served with potatoes and parsley sauce). Like coffee, these items introduced in the upper class eventually became part of everyday cuisine for the entire populace.

It was around 1700 that the *æbleskiver* pan as we known it today was developed. A traditional Danish dessert that probably dates back to the middle ages, *æbleskiver* (literally, "apple slices") are doughnut-like balls made with a mixture similar to pancake batter (see recipe, p. 61). They began in a time when most Danish homes did not have ovens, which meant that dishes that could be fried on the stovetop—such as waffles, pancakes, and *æbleskiver*—were most practical. *Æbleskiver* became a favorite holiday treat in Denmark, and are mentioned in a Hans Christian Andersen holiday story from 1872 as well as the classic *"Peters Jul"* ("Peter's Christmas").

Peasants lived in villages and tilled the land jointly in an open-field system into the 20th century. But in the late 1700s, agricultural reforms allowed

A special stovetop pan with round indentations used to make the Danish specialty called *æbleskiver*. Illustration by Pietro Krohn in *"Peters Jul,"* 1889.

farmers to own parcels of land. These newly independent farmers who moved out onto the land itself would later be important in the cooperative movement.

In 1807, during the Napoleonic Wars, Copenhagen sustained considerable damage when bombarded by the English army during a battle in which the British hoped to seize the Danish navy's sizable fleet. Seven years later a defeated and bankrupt Denmark ceded Norway to Sweden, a union that lasted until Norway gained its independence in 1905.

The new borders for Denmark included only what is now Denmark itself and the duchies of Slesvig and Holstein. (These duchies were lost to Germany in 1864, reducing Denmark again by one third.) The many years of war bankrupted the country in 1813, and widespread famine followed.

This national crisis led to major changes in industrialization and agriculture. The Danish government set to work to strengthen Danish agriculture through education and research, and by the end of the 19th century Denmark was self-sufficient in food production. "Today we produce enough food products for 30 million people, even though Denmark's population is only just over 5 million," Per Holten-Andersen stated with pride while dean of Landbohøjskolen (now called the University of Copenhagen Faculty of Life Sciences).

The signing of the constitution of Denmark on June 5, 1849, marked the country's peaceful transition from absolutism to constitutional monarchy, establishing the two houses of parliament, albeit with only propertied male members. The constitution created that year defines the rights and privileges of the Danish citizens, including freedom of expression and freedom of assembly. In 1915 voting rights were extended to all women as well as non-propertied men. June 5 is celebrated annually as *Grundlovsdag* (Constitution Day), with political rallies to mark the occasion.

Agricultural Reform in the Late 19th Century

An influx of grain from the New World and the Ukraine during the late 19th century (called "the grain invasion") led to a decline in prices for grain exports. Danish farmers responded by switching their primary production from grain to dairy products and meat. The infrastructure required to process these products—dairies and slaughterhouses—inspired the formation of the Danish agricultural cooperative movement, called *andelsbevægelse*, in which groups of farmers invest in shared facilities and joint marketing efforts. Today more than 90 percent of the total production of meat and dairy in Denmark is from farmer-owned cooperatives. Lurpak Butter and Danish Bacon are successful agricultural companies that are outgrowths of this important movement. Grocery stores such as Brugsen are also cooperatives, as are some of Denmark's wind power companies.

Several major changes in Danish diet appeared in the 18th and 19th centuries. Considering that today potatoes are a staple in traditional Danish cuisine, it is surprising to discover that they were not grown in Denmark until the early 1700s. Potatoes were introduced to Danish farmers at that time by the French Huguenots, who had imported the potato from South America in the 16th century. Frederik IV (1671 to 1730) had invited the French Huguenots to seek refuge in Denmark in 1720 after they had lost their right to practice their religion at home. Some years later, in 1759, Frederik V (1723 to 1766) recruited Germans—later known as potato Germans—to come to Denmark to cultivate potatoes in Jutland. The moors of central and western Jutland had been abandoned as farmland after the plague, called the Black Death, had decimated the Danish population in the 14th century, but the sandy soils there proved hospitable to this new crop.

Smørrebrød, the popular Danish open-faced sandwiches, are usually considered to date back to the 1840s when workers and farm laborers needing to pack a lunch discovered that it was easy to take a flat piece of bread and put meat, cheese, or fish on it. But they may actually date back to the Middle Ages, when bread was used as a plate, or to a later time when bread was used to wipe plates clean of any remaining food. In 1883 Restaurant Nimb in Copenhagen's Tivoli Gardens became the first restaurant to offer fancy *smørrebrød* on its menu. Oskar Davidsen started to offer *smørrebrød* in his *vinstue* (wine bar) in 1888, and his list of open-faced sandwiches eventually grew to 178—with a checklist over four feet long for placing orders. See *Tastes of Denmark* (p. 47) for some modern *smørrebrød* recipes.

In the 1950s even passengers traveling by air on SAS enjoyed freshly made *smørrebrød*. Photo from *Insider's Guide to Smørrebrød* used with permission of Ole Troelsø.

Beer became a significant export for Denmark after J. C. Jacobsen, the owner of Carlsberg, bred a new strain of lager yeast in 1847 that allowed breweries to produce a larger, consistent output. The Danish brewery Tuborg, which was founded in 1873, was acquired by its rival in 1970, and today Carlsberg is the fourth largest brewery group in the world.

Bakers in Denmark were originally divided between those that baked bread (*bagere*) and the few that made cakes and pastries (*konditorer*). But in the 1800s, the lines between the two began to blur as sweets became increasingly popular throughout the country. At the same time, home baking became possible thanks to cast-iron stoves. Danes have been getting together for coffee and pastries ever since.

Perhaps the best-known food item from Denmark is the flaky pastry with a filling of jam, marzipan, or custard (or in the US, sweet bakers' cheese) referred to around the world as a Danish. In its traditional pretzel shape, used as a shop sign to indicate a bakery, it is called a *kringle*. The story is often repeated that in 1850 the Danish Confectioners, Bakers and Chocolate Makers Association went on strike, forcing bakery owners to hire foreign workers. Among these were Austrian bakers who brought with them their own recipe for a puff pastry called *plundergebäck*. When the strike ended these pastries continued to be made, and to this day they are called *wienerbrød* (Vienna bread) in Denmark— and Danish everywhere else. The late food historian Bi Skaarup credited

Copenhagen baker Niels Christian Albeck, who studied in Vienna in 1845, with the introduction of *wienerbrød* to Danish culture. She wrote that King Christian VIII and Queen Caroline Amalie insisted on daily deliveries of the pastry that Albeck developed by combining Viennese puff pastry with a sugared filling. It soon became so popular that many other Copenhagen bakeries were making their own versions.

In the 1840s cast-iron stoves made it possible for many households to have their own ovens, which previously had been outlawed due to fire hazard. This made it easy for the home baker to make cookies and other baked desserts, and according to Skaarup Danish favorites such as the *vaniljekrans*, the forerunner of Denmark's famous butter cookie, date to this period. Find a recipe for these vanilla wreath cookies on page 67.

Denmark in Recent Times

The 20th century saw a flourishing of agriculture in Denmark, aided by the cooperative movement. However there was also continued migration into the cities for industrial jobs, which meant that food markets and restaurants multiplied in urban areas to serve this growing populace. In a quintessentially Danish movement that started in the late 1800s and continues to flourish today, thousands of Danes in cities were able to keep a connection with the land through *kolonihaver*, or allotment gardens. These areas are mostly owned by municipalities and rented to allotment societies, which in turn divide them into small plots that provide their members with a bit of land for a garden and a place to relax outside the city. Most allotment gardens today have a tiny house or shed on them, and are used for socializing as well as for gardening.

Denmark remained neutral in World War I, and some Danish factories did a thriving business in canned food provided to the troops from Germany and other countries during the war. The factory owners were known as *Gullaschbaroner* (goulash barons) because they earned so much money selling canned

The *kringle*-shaped bakery sign used today originated in the seal of the bakers's guild in the 1600s.

food—especially beef goulash—during wartime. Exports of meat soared during this period. However many of those who profited from the trade went bankrupt during the following decade.

Like many other countries, Denmark suffered greatly under the Great Depression in the 1930s. The depressed economy in Great Britain, which had been buying 750 tons of bacon a week from the Danish Bacon Company, caused a crisis in Danish pork production. When the British parliament imposed a quota system on pork imports in order to protect their own farmers, the Danish government was forced to curtail pork production in Denmark. In 1933 farmers were issued licenses (called "pig cards") based on their previous production and their farm size. Industries other than agriculture were also impacted, and at one time Danish unemployment reached 32 percent. This inspired the laws that led Denmark to be known today as a welfare state where all citizens have equal rights to social security.

During World War II Denmark's neutrality was breached by German troops, who occupied the country starting in the spring of 1940. The five years of occupation brought real hardship to the Danes, including food shortages and rationing. Farmers had difficulty in obtaining grain to feed their livestock, and were entirely cut off from their primary markets for pork and butter in Great Britain.

The trying years of the Depression and the occupation made it necessary for porridge or gruel to be a staple in many evening meals. *Øllebrød* (porridge made of beer and *rugbrød*) served with milk or cream is a uniquely Danish dish that was both filling and made good use of every last piece of a loaf of bread. It experienced a revival recently when the famous restaurant Noma created its own version of this traditional dish.

After the war, Denmark received financial assistance from the Marshall Plan to help to modernize its agriculture and industry. The new prosperity of the second half of the century saw women entering the workforce in greater numbers than before, which in turn contributed to the rise of convenience food. Frozen food became especially popular both for the home cook and as an export.

In the late 1950s the thriving export of Danish butter to England declined somewhat, leading to a surplus in Denmark. In order to increase the use of dairy products in the home market, artist Grete Rich of Aarhus was asked to design a mascot for the Danish dairy industry. The result was Karoline the Cow, a cheerful red and white cow (originally made from a pair of gingham checked curtains). She made her debut in Copenhagen's Tivoli Gardens in

Karoline the Cow, the mascot of the Danish dairy industry, was created in 1958. Arla Foods acquired Karolines Køkken (Karoline's Kitchen), a division that offers home cooks easy-to-prepare recipes, in 2003. Image courtesy of the Danish Dairy Board.

1958, and in the coming decades was represented by Karoline Girls traveling around the country and abroad giving demonstrations of the many ways to use Danish milk, butter, and other dairy products.

The export of bacon to England is one reason for the popularity of *leverpostej*, the liver pâté that is a favorite traditional *smørrebrød* topping. Processing pigs for bacon makes a lot of pork livers available, so the Danes developed a strong affinity for *leverpostej*. In fact, at one time Danish children could expect at least one of the open-faced sandwiches in their school lunch to be made with *leverpostej,* which was as common as peanut butter and jelly sandwiches were to American students.

As the century progressed and Danes traveled more widely, they became interested in other cuisines. Gourmet French food became the standard for fine dining in Danish restaurants, rather than traditional Danish foods. According to Bi Skaarup, "In the 1990s Danish cuisine was declining. Danes looked at price, not quality. Also, if you wanted to eat good food you ate Spanish, French, or other cuisines."

Another factor in the decline of traditional Danish foods was the influx of guest workers, especially between the late 1960s and 1973, and the immigrants who came after Denmark joined the European Union. These immigrants introduced the foods and spices of their home country in what had been a relatively homogenous national cusine. Today immigrants and their descendants constitute about 10 percent of the population, with the largest group coming from Turkey, followed by Poland, Germany, and Iraq.

A Revitalization of Danish Cuisine

The early 21st century saw the birth of the New Nordic Cuisine movement, a renewal of interest in traditional Scandinavian foods. Inspired by the Slow Food movement elsewhere in the world, it encourages the use of fresh, organic, and locally sourced ingredients both in home cooking and restaurants. Danish chefs René Redzepi and Claus Meyer opened the restaurant Noma in Copenhagen (Noma stands for *Nordisk Mad*, which means "Nordic Food") in 2004. They also gathered chefs from all over Scandinavia to discuss how to develop a cuisine that emphasizes "purity, simplicity, and freshness" and the increased use of seasonal foods to develop traditional dishes using ingredients that benefit from the local region's terroir: climate, water, and soil. The result is the ten-point "Manifesto for the New Nordic Kitchen," an important document that serves as a reference point for a movement that, in typical Danish fashion, is democratic and open to everyone.

According to Rasmus Kofoed, the award-winning chef who is co-owner of Geranium in Copenhagen, traditional Danish food was very high in fat and very rich. The New Nordic movement takes the same local ingredients and makes dishes that are lighter, fresher, and more flavorful. In response to this movement, the city of Copenhagen created a new Torvehallerne on the site of the city's market square. This year-round facility includes both indoor and outdoor vendors, and is a great place for visitors to explore the wide range of Danish produce, fish, cheese, meats, preserves, baked goods, wine, and beer. There is even a shop specializing in products from the island of Bornholm. The two year-round buildings include a variety of restaurants and takeaway options, and the outdoor stalls feature vegetables and fruits from around the country during the growing season.

Organic food in Denmark is increasingly popular thanks to the New Nordic Cuisine. Its principles of purity, animal welfare, and sustainability are in harmony with the principles of the organic food movement. Today Danes consume more organic products per capita than any other country in the world, in part because organic production has been made a priority by the Danish government. Denmark was the first country in the world to establish regulations governing organic food production and official inspections of organic foodstuffs and producers. The government further supports organic agriculture by purchasing organic products for public sector institutions such as preschools and kindergartens, and homes for the elderly.

Scientists at the University of Copenhagen have been studying traditional Scandinavian cuisine and its contemporary incarnation as New Nordic Cuisine, and have found the Nordic Diet to have great potential as a healthy way of eating. The emphasis is on local, seasonal organic foods including fish, wild game, whole grain *rugbrød*, potatoes, fresh vegetables, nuts, berries, and fruits. The Nordic Diet seeks to limit processed foods, sugar, and fat, as well as the pork and butter that have been key elements in Danish cuisine because of their importance in Danish agriculture.

Everyone agrees that the rising popularity of Nordic cuisine is due in large part to Noma, the small restaurant on the Christianshavn waterfront that gained widespread fame when it was selected as the Best Restaurant in the World three years in a row starting in 2010. This recognition has helped spread interest in the New Nordic Cuisine internationally, and has made Denmark a culinary travel destination for the first time. Visitors to Denmark today enjoy a wide range of foods, from traditional *smørrebrød* to Japanese sushi (and even the Royal Cafe's creative combination of the two, which are called *smushi*). They can find foods dating back to the time of the Vikings, traditional dishes known as *mormormad* (food from grandmother's time), and the latest New Nordic dishes. The trend is for chefs to use domestic ingredients, some freshly foraged from the fields, forests, and marshes, or harvested from the North Sea, as they create versions of traditional Danish specialties unique to our time.

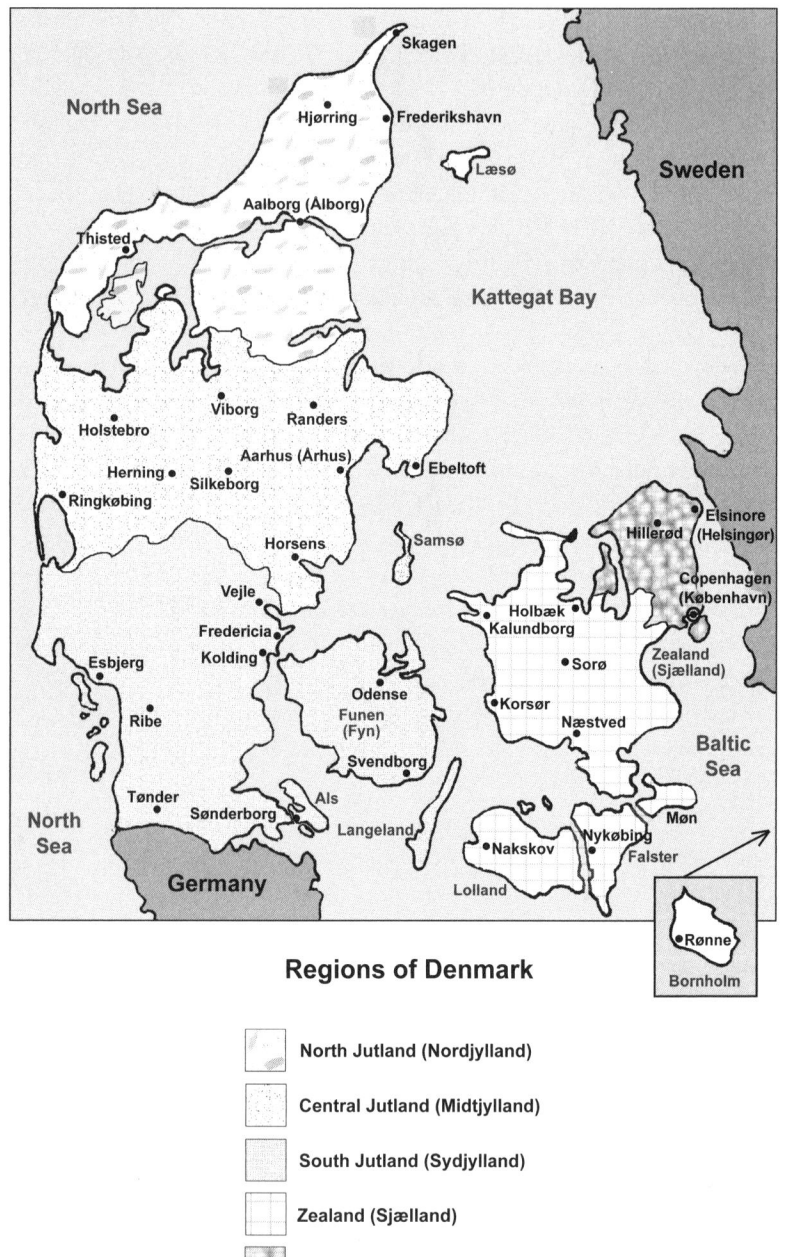

Regions of Denmark

- North Jutland (Nordjylland)
- Central Jutland (Midtjylland)
- South Jutland (Sydjylland)
- Zealand (Sjælland)
- Capital Region (Hovestaden)

Regional Danish Food

A Quick Tour of Danish Foods and Their Regional Variations

Danish Food in a Nutshell

Danish cuisine has been undergoing a revolution since the last decade of the 20th century. When we asked three school children on a train in Denmark about their favorite food, two of them answered, "pasta," and the third answered, "tortillas." And a women's magazine surveying the most popular foods in Denmark recently put pizza in first place and pasta with meat sauce, a dish which would have been unheard of not that long ago, in third. So while we acknowledge that dining options in Denmark have become very international, we also realize that most people already know how to order a pizza, spaghetti, or a taco. Our goal in this chapter is to introduce you to foods that are traditionally Danish.

Smørrebrød, which literally means "buttered bread," are the open-faced sandwiches considered by many to be the ultimate Danish national dish. *Smørrebrød* traditionally begin by taking a piece of bread—most often Danish *rugbrød* (a dense pumpernickel rye bread sliced very thin; see recipe, p. 45), but sometimes white or French bread—covering it with a layer of either butter or lard, and then adding various main toppings, referred to collectively as *pålæg*, and the appropriate garnishes. Some of the more traditional *smørrebrød* combinations include marinated herring on *rugbrød* with chopped onions, *fjordrejer* (tiny fjord shrimp) on white bread with mayonnaise and lemon, and *leverpostej* (pork liver pâté; see recipe, p. 49) on *rugbrød* with sliced pickled beets or bacon. Other traditional favorites on *rugbrød* include roast beef with grated horseradish and *remoulade* (see recipe, p. 58), *frikadeller* (meatballs; see recipe, p. 48) with red cabbage, roast pork with pickled cucumbers, and boiled potatoes with mayonnaise and crispy onions.

Danish *smørrebrød* can be as simple as one piece of bread with butter and one topping or as complex as a towering work of art made up of a half dozen toppings, each of which requires time and effort to prepare. They are often decorated with garnishes such as *agurkesalat* (cucumber salad; see recipe, p. 57), *rødkål* (pickled red cabbage; see recipe, p. 59), chives, onion, radish, or lemon. Some are named by listing the toppings included, but others have more creative names such as *dyrlaegens natmad*, meaning "the veterinarian's nighttime snack" (see recipe, p. 47), and *stjerneskud*, meaning "shooting star" (see recipe, p. 50).

Smørrebrød are traditionally eaten at lunch, and one can even purchase a special *smørrebrød* lunchbox that is just the right size for four thin slices of *rugbrød* with toppings. And although a good, piled-high *smørrebrød* with toppings that completely hide the bread must be eaten with a knife and fork, a more modest *smørrebrød* packed for a school or work lunch box is considered to be a *håndmad* ("hand meal") and is eaten without utensils. Children (and some adults!) enjoy finishing their lunch with a chocolate *smørrebrød* made by topping a piece of *rugbrød* with a thin layer of butter and a piece of *pålægschokolade* (wafer-thin rectangles of milk or dark chocolate). The nutritional value of the *rugbrød* makes this a healthy dessert option.

Many of the countless toppings that can be used to make *smørrebrød* are leftovers or kitchen staples common throughout Denmark, such as cold potatoes, *spegepølse* (salami), *leverpostej*, and bacon. A casual lunch might involve a variety of toppings and garnishes being put on the table for guests to make their own sandwiches, or the *smørrebrød* might be served ready-made. There are many complex combinations of toppings and garnishes considered to be classics. In earlier times several years of training went into learning to be a professional "*smørrebrød* maiden," a cook who specialized in these cold dishes (in contrast to a "warm maiden," whose specialty was hot entrées).

Another quick lunch option in Denmark is a hot dog from the once-omnipresent Danish *pølsevogn* (hot dog stand). These have been a national fixture for over a century, and there is even one in the baggage claim area in the Copenhagen airport for travelers who are homesick for hot dogs. These stands all offer a wide variety of sausages, so it's good to know the options before placing your order. Start by taking a look at the poster menu, complete with photos, displayed on the front of the *pølsevogn*. The following descriptions should prove helpful in deciphering all the different types of hot dogs. Keep in mind that most of them are pork based—but if you don't really want a pork sausage, there is usually at least one burger sandwich on the

Hot dog stands are a common sight on the streets of most Danish cities. Photo courtesy of the Tulip Food Company.

menu. Vegetarians, on the other hand, are pretty much out of luck unless there is a falafel stand nearby. Stands offering falafel and shawarma (a popular Middle Eastern meat sandwich) are becoming increasingly common sights, and have replaced many of the traditional Danish hot dog stands.

The basic *rød pølse* (red sausage) is a long, skinny, bright-red hot dog. This boiled sausage, which is unique to Denmark, is traditionally served at children's birthday parties. A *pølse* on a bun, instead of having the bread served alongside it, is called a *hotdog*. A *hotdog* is either a boiled *rød pølse* or a *ristet* (grilled) sausage called a *wienerpølse*. A *fransk hotdog* (French hot dog) comes inserted into the center of a hollowed-out baguette already seasoned with a tangy mayonnaise sauce. You can also choose a *medisterpølse* (similar to a coarsely textured bratwurst), or a large frankfurter (a type of bratwurst). Some sausages, including the classic *rød pølse*, are served with a roll on the side, which is indicated on the sign as *m. brød* (with bread) or *m. pølsebrød* (with a hot dog roll). If you see *i svøb* (in swaddling), that means that the hot dog is wrapped in bacon. A *kradser* (scratcher), which is bread with the condiments but without any sausage, is the only vegetarian option at a *pølsevogn*. It is probably called a "scratcher" because it scratches all the way down your throat.

The standard accompaniments for a *rød pølse* are sweet *ketchup* (catsup) and spicy *sennep* (mustard), usually squirted alongside the sausage on a piece of waxed paper, and you may also ask for *ristede løg* (crispy onions). If you choose a sausage that comes in a bun, crispy onions or *rå løg* (raw onions) and *syltede agurker* (cucumber salad) are great toppings. Another option is the popular Danish sauce called *remoulade*, which is a bit like a sweet tartar sauce made with mayonnaise, chopped pickles, capers, and mustard. *Remoulade* appears on the Danish menu on top of roast beef *smørrebrød* and also alongside fried fish.

If you've never eaten a hot dog that didn't come in a bun, you may wonder about how to proceed. Most people hold the sausage in their fingers and dip it in the catsup and mustard before taking a take a bite, then intersperse the bites of sausage with bites of the roll. But this is street food, so there is no fancy etiquette involved.

Denmark is known around the world for its cheese, which is eaten both for breakfast and as a topping on *smørrebrød*. The climate and soil of Denmark are almost ideal for dairy cattle farming, with relatively high temperatures in the spring and summer, mild winters, even rainfall throughout the year, and fertile soil for grazing. The result is a thriving dairy industry that accounts for 20% of Danish agricultural exports, including both cheese and butter. There are many specialty cheeses produced for export and for domestic consumption, including blue cheese, Havarti, Danbo, Esrom, and Maribo. These cheeses range from Danablu, a cow's milk blue cheese recognized by the EU as being uniquely Danish, to slicing cheeses that range from mild to quite "smelly." Remember to start with milder cheeses when tasting them in a cheese shop, because a really strong cheese such as the Danbo called Gamle Ole ("old Ole") can literally numb your taste buds.

Pork was for many years the most popular meat in Denmark, often eaten with thick brown gravy. The main course might feature *frikadeller* (meatballs of ground veal and pork sautéed in butter; see recipe, p. 48), a national favorite that dates back to the 1200s, *langtidsbraiseret svineskank* (braised pork shank; see recipe, p. 55), or *medister pølse* (pork sausage). *Stegt flæsk med persillesovs* (slices of fried pork belly served with potatoes in a white sauce with parsley) is another favorite, especially at casual restaurants. For a special occasion such as Christmas dinner, *flæskesteg med svær* (pork roast with the crackling) may be served. Unfortunately for those trying to recreate this dish in the US, the required cut of meat is almost impossible to find except at specialty butcher shops.

Danish bacon, which resembles Canadian bacon, is a popular garnish on *smørrebrød* and is also used as an ingredient in other dishes. But a large percentage of Danish bacon is exported, especially to Great Britain and the continent. Today it is often shipped out as pork and cured into bacon in other countries, often in Germany and Poland.

Skipperlabskovs (a stew of cubed beef or pork, onion, and potatoes; see recipe, p. 55) is a traditional dish, originally from northern Germany, made popular by the restaurant Grøften in Tivoli. Tivoli Gardens is the second oldest amusement park in the world, and is located right in the center of Copenhagen. Grøften opened in 1887, not long after Tivoli itself, and is famous for its *fjordrejer* (tiny fjord shrimp) and its *skipperlabskovs*—of which it sells 50 tons each year.

Ground beef is still sometimes served raw in Denmark in an elegant beef tartar *smørrebrød*, and is also used to make *hakkebøf* (a beef patty served with slightly caramelized onions) and *Pariser bøf* (which is served on top of a piece of white bread, often with a raw egg yolk). Beef roasts and steak are also sometimes served as the main course, and the Danes use the English words for rare, medium, and well-done. Today chicken is a much more popular entrée than in the past, when it was considered a treat because it was

more expensive than pork. Sunday dinner might have been *gammeldags kylling* (old-fashioned braised chicken; see recipe, p. 56), which is still a favorite dish.

Herring is a national specialty, and is usually served as the first course in a lunch of *smørrebrød*. It might be smoked, fried, pickled, or in a sauce, always on top of a piece of *rugbrød*. Fish entrées often feature the day's catch, and even chain grocery stores have excellent fresh fish counters offering local fish such as *torsk* (cod), *rødspætte* (European plaice), salmon, sea trout, and garfish. Popular seafood dishes include fried plaice or poached, fried, or baked cod (see recipe, p. 55). *Ål* (eel), which is considered a delicacy served smoked or fried, is in increasingly short supply.

Fiskerkonen, a sculpture by Charles Svejstrup Madsen erected in the Copenhagen harbor market Gammel Strand in 1940. It depicts a fisherman's wife selling fresh-caught European plaice (*rødspætte*).

23

You might not expect to find curry in Danish cuisine, but *boller i karry* (pork meatballs in a very mild curry sauce) is one of the most popular dishes in the country, especially for families with children. *Boller i karry* is served on rice, which is unusual in traditional Danish cuisine. The potato is such a central feature of traditional Danish dinners that this is one of the few meals that doesn't include either rye bread or potatoes—or both. Curry powder, introduced in Denmark by the British in 1828, is also used in *karrysild* (curried herring; see recipe, p. 47) and *karrytorsk* (cod in a curry sauce).

Vegetables in Denmark tend to be used as garnishes on *smørrebrød*, or served as a side dish—especially the omnipresent pickled beets, red cabbage, and pickled cucumber salad. Carrots, tomatoes, cabbage, kale, lettuce, radishes, and asparagus are popular locally grown produce, much of which is raised organically.

Danish pastry is another specialty known around the world. This flaky pastry is made by folding many layers of dough and butter together, and it is rare for a home baker to attempt this time-consuming process—especially when the country abounds with bakeries and *konditorier* (fancier pastry bakeries) selling freshly made breads, cakes, pastries, and cookies.

Many Danish desserts, drinks, and even entrées take advantage of the wild and cultivated berries and fruits found throughout the country, including apples, rhubarb, strawberries, and raspberries, as well as *stikkelsbær* (gooseberries), *ribs* (red currants), and *solbær* (black currants). *Hyben* (rosehips) can be harvested in many coastal areas, and are used in jelly and jam. *Hyldebær* (elderberry, *Sambucus nigra*) is a berry that is also used to make jam, although they are mildly poisonous when unripe. The elderberry flower—*hyldeblomst*—is used to make a delicious fruit drink concentrate, which is served mixed with water.

It's no accident that Denmark ranks as one of the top ice-cream eating countries in the world. There are ice cream stands everywhere during the precious months of warm, long summer days. You can take the easy way out and choose one of the many Popsicle-type treats clearly pictured on the poster in every kiosk and ice cream stand. But if you want real ice cream, you'll have to decide between *softis* (soft-serve) or old-fashioned scooped ice cream. If you do order soft-serve, your next choices are fairly simple. You specify the size you want, from reasonable to gigantic. There are usually just a few flavors to choose from—although you may find licorice here, as well as in old-fashioned ice cream—and you can add *drys* (sprinkles) if you like. Chocolate is the normal flavor of *drys*, but you may come across Harlequin *drys* in the bright colors of the famed Tivoli pantomime theater, and there is even licorice *drys.*

If you want old-fashioned ice cream, the first question will be how many *kugler* (balls or scoops) you want as the base for your creation, and of course what flavors you'd like them each to be. Any flavor is sure to be delicious, because they're all made with fresh Danish cream. Then you'll need to decide if you want *guf* on your cone. If you're going to order the perfect *gammeldags is* ("old-fashioned" ice cream cone) in Denmark, you need to know that *guf*— which can refer to anything yummy to eat, especially candy and cakes—in this case refers to a creamy substance that covers the entire cone like molten lava. This topping, made by mixing whipped egg whites with sugar, is a bit like marshmallow fluff.

An alternative to *guf* as a base for the sprinkles on your cone is whipped cream, and although it is not sweetened as it is in the US, it does make the cone more like an ice cream sundae. Instead of a cherry on top, the Danes add two more key ingredients: a dollop of strawberry jam and a chocolate-coated marshmallow treat called a *flødebolle.* Jam is such a popular feature on traditional cones that some ice cream stands have a squirt container hanging at the ready from the ceiling. But jam doesn't come close to the national obsession with the *flødebolle*, which is similar to a Mallomar cookie but with a thin wafer bottom. Denmark claims to be the country where the *flødebolle* originated in the early 1800s, and today it produces approximately 800 million of these chocolate-coated treats every year, many of them destined for the top of an old-fashioned ice cream cone.

Candy has a long tradition in Denmark, and Anthon Berg has been making fine chocolates in Copenhagen since 1884. They are known for their dark chocolates with marzipan fillings, as well as little chocolate bottles filled with well-known liqueurs (keep in mind that these have an alcoholic content of up to 5%). Gummy candy is a favorite of Danish children, and in fact the amusement park called BonBon-Land takes the names of its rides from one company's gummies with off-color names such as "dirty diaper" and "rat poop."

Colorful hard candy is available in many different flavors, often sold by the pound. One can visit Sømods Bolcher on Nørregade in Copenhagen to watch them pull and cut boiled sugar hard candy in the same way that they've been making it since 1891. If you're lucky, they'll stop and offer you a taste—and it may not be licorice! Make sure to buy a sample of a variety of flavors, from *rabarber* (rhubarb) to *hyldeblomst* (elderflower). You can even bring home little candies with the Danish flag in the center as a souvenir.

Danes love their salty, strong licorice, which is sometimes called *salmiak lakrids* in reference to the ammonium chloride (*salmiak*) that gives the candy its special taste.

While many types of candy are popular in Denmark, you can't go anywhere in the country without seeing copious amounts of black licorice. Danes consume over 600 million of just one type of licorice *pastilles* (Ga-Jol) per year. Danish black licorice is different from American licorice. It is called *saltlakrids* (salt licorice) and has a very distinctive taste due to the ammonium chloride that is added to the licorice root. Licorice can be purchased at any grocery store or candy store and comes in a variety of shapes, sizes, and textures, such as small hard candies or a gummy roll. At Tivoli, try the freshly made licorice lollipop, which will harden as you lick it—if you can handle the somewhat overpowering taste! However if you do enjoy the strong Danish licorice, the FDA warns not to overindulge. Danish licorice is extremely high in sodium, and the compound glycyrrhizin, which is found in licorice root, can temporarily increase blood pressure levels.

The Regions of Denmark

Danish cuisine, like the country's population, has until recent times been fairly homogenous. Asking Danes about local specialties brings responses ranging from the specifics of what type of cabbage is served on Christmas Eve to the number of cookies and cakes offered with coffee. But throughout the country, cabbage is traditionally served on Christmas Eve, and cookies and cakes are offered with coffee.

There are, however, a few ways in which food and culinary traditions help define the local culture of the different Danish regions, as well as some of the 70 small islands that are inhabited. Denmark's regional specialties usually depend on the foods and ingredients that are easily grown or found in that geographic area. For example, towns closer to the sea have a greater emphasis on fish than those that are farther inland. Similarly, the area of Jutland that borders Germany has food specialties more closely related to northern German cuisine.

Denmark was officially divided into five regions in 2007, replacing the thirteen former counties. These regions are the Capital Region (*Hovedstaden*), including Copenhagen and the northern part of the island of Zealand, plus Bornholm; Zealand (*Sjaelland*), including the southern part of Zealand and the islands of Møn, Falster, and Lolland; Southern Denmark (*Syddanmark*), including Funen, Ærø, Langeland, and the southern part of Jutland; Central Jutland (*Midtjylland*); and North Jutland (*Nordjylland*). Many Danes—and tourists—still refer to the main regions of Denmark by the name of the island or area, the four largest being the island of Zealand (where Copenhagen is located), the island of Funen (largest city: Odense), the Jutland peninsula (largest city: Aarhus), and the island of Bornholm. These four simplified geographical regions also provide the best framework for understanding the regional differences in the cuisine of Denmark.

The Island of Zealand

Zealand (*Sjælland*) is the biggest Danish island, and is home to about half the country's population. Copenhagen (*København*) is both the capital and the largest Danish city. But not far outside Copenhagen and its suburbs, fishing, dairy farming, cattle breeding, and the cultivation of grains and vegetables are still of great economic—and culinary—importance on this 2,700 square mile island.

The northern coast of Zealand is home to several picturesque fishing villages where it is possible to eat freshly caught seafood. And two of Denmark's best-known cheeses come from this region. Dairy farmer Hanne Nielsen is credited with creating Havarti in 1870 and naming it after her farm, Havarthigaard, near Øverød in northern Zealand. This semi-soft cheese can still be found in Denmark and around the world, with optional flavorings ranging from dill to cranberry to complement its mild creamy flavor.

In 1874 Hanne Nielsen also created an early version of Danish blue cheese, a semi-soft blue-veined creamery cheese. She hoped to produce a cheese similar to Roquefort, a blue-veined sheep's milk cheese she had encountered on a study trip abroad. Forty years later dairyman Marius Boel perfected Danablu, the cow's milk blue cheese now recognized by the EU as being uniquely Danish. Before a block of Danablu is aged, copper wires or rods are inserted to pierce the formed curds and distribute the *Penicillium roqueforti* mold evenly. Danablu has a yellowish edible rind, a 25–30% fat content, and a mild flavor with a characteristic sharp, salty taste. In Denmark it is often eaten on bread or biscuits.

Copenhagen is known for its longstanding tradition of fine bakeries, including Conditori La Glace. This *konditori* (pastry shop) dates back to 1870, and is the home of many famous cakes including the *sportskage* (literally, "sports cake"), made of crushed nougat, whipped cream, a macaroon bottom, and caramelized choux pastry, and the *Othellokage* (Othello cake) with custard cream, a macaroon bottom, sponge cake layers, and chocolate glaze. Visitors to the legendary La Glace may wish to share a piece of these very rich creations.

Marianne Stagetorn Kolos, owner of Conditori La Glace, shows off the bakery's famous *sportskage* (sports cake). It's not a cake for athletes—the name comes from a late 19th-century play called "The Sportsmen."

The city is also the birthplace of the New Nordic Cuisine food movement, with its revolutionary approach to reinventing traditional foods using the freshest local ingredients—some of which are foraged in the forests and coastal areas of Zealand, or caught in the waters of the North Sea.

The islands of Møn, Falster, and Lolland, located south of Zealand, are of agricultural significance, and the orchards in this area are known for their pears and apples. It is said that the best apple juice and cider in Denmark come from this region.

Møn is known for a local specialty called *bidesild og fedtemad* ("bite" herring and fat-covered bread). Brined herring are eaten straight out of the salt barrel together with rings of raw onion and pieces of *rugbrød* covered with a thick layer of pork fat. Needless to say, a lot of beer is required to accompany this "men's" dish. Another Møn specialty is *hvedekage* (which means "wheat cake," although it is actually a bread made with refined flour) served with cheese and homemade pickled plums for lunch or coffee.

The islands of Lolland and Falster are known for a soup called *mælkeærter*, which means "milk peas." This summer dish is made from milk, carrots, cubed potatoes, and of course peas. It is served with smoked bacon on the side.

The Island of Funen

The island of Funen (*Fyn*) is famous for the fact that Odense, its largest city, is the birthplace of Hans Christian Andersen (known in Denmark as H. C. Andersen). But it is also an agricultural area with a mild climate that makes it ideal for growing vegetables and fruits, including strawberries, apples, and cherries. The farms of Funen produce meats, including lamb, veal, and pork, and regional delicacies include local sausages and other cold cuts.

Funen's signature food is a smoked creamy cheese called *rygeost* (literally "smoked cheese"). Some say that *rygeost* is the only truly original Danish cheese. *Rygeost* is produced by combining regular cow's milk with buttermilk, then adding rennet to let it form curds. The cheeses are smoked over a straw and nettle fire and frequently coated with cumin or caraway seeds to give them a distinct flavor. *Rygeost* can be used in salad dressing or mixed with mayonnaise and served with sliced radishes on *rugbrød*.

The type of coffee cake known as *brunsviger* is considered a specialty of Funen, even though the name probably comes from the German city of Braunschweig. To make *brunsviger*, a soft yeast dough is topped with a *remonce* (Danish pastry filling) made of brown sugar and butter, and holes are poked into the dough to let the filling sink in during baking. *Brunsviger* is a Sunday morning treat, and this type of dough is also used to make a birthday cake for young children shaped like a man (*kageman*) or woman (*kagekone*).

A person from Funen is called a *Fynbo*, which is the origin of the name of another cheese closely associated with the island. Fynbo is a semi-hard cheese with a natural golden exterior and cream-colored interior. It has a taste similar to Gouda or Monterey Jack, with an aroma of cooked buckwheat. Pasteurized cow's milk and animal rennet are used to make the cheese, which is then shaped into cylinders and aged for several months. Fynbo is still produced in small quantities on the island of Funen, and is used throughout Denmark on open-faced sandwiches and on bread at breakfast.

One of the specialties of Funen is a version of *æbleflæsk* (apple pork), slices and cubes of fried pork or bacon served with slices of apples fried in the same fat. Another is *æggekage* (a Danish omelette; see recipe, p. 53), which has been served at Restaurant Carlslund in Odense since 1860. This egg dish is topped with both bacon and fried pork rinds and is served in large, *ad libitum* (all-you-can-eat) portions.

Odense is home to the internationally known almond paste producer Odense Marcipan. Bookkeeper Lauritz Thobo-Carlsen purchased a little *marcipan* (marzipan) business there in 1909, and built up the business by selling marzipan to Danish bakers needing increasingly large quantities for marzipan pastries when they became the fashion in the 1930s. Several of these, including one called a *Napoleonshat* (Napoleon's hat) and *mazarinkage* (see recipe, p. 65) are still found in most *konditorier* (fancy bakeries) today. This type of Danish pastry is called a *tørkage* (dry cake), because it doesn't include whipped cream.

In addition to marzipan, Odense Marcipan now manufactures nougat, chocolate, and dough for making the traditional Danish wedding and New

Year's Eve cake called a *kransekage* (wreath cake). Progressive sizes of rings of *kransekage*, which is made of baked almond paste dough, are lightly iced and assembled either in the form of a tower or an *overflødighedshorn* (cornucopia). It is traditional to decorate the *kransekage* with small Danish flags. When shaped like a cornucopia, the *kransekage* is often filled with chocolates, candies, or small cookies, and used for confirmations and other special occasions.

Chef John Kofod Pedersen of Sortebro Kro in Odense with his special Funen salad featuring poached eggs and a *rygeøst* dressing.

The Jutland Peninsula

South Jutland, an area also known as the Region of Southern Denmark, is located between the North Sea and the Baltic. It is here that the peninsula connects Denmark with the rest of Europe, and its southern border with Germany has been the subject of many conflicts over the years. Today part of the border area, historically known as Slesvig-Holsten, is divided between Germany (Holstein and the southern part of Schleswig, to use their German names) and Denmark (the northern part of Slesvig). However there are German- and Danish-speaking residents in both parts of Slesvig-Holsten, and the two cultures—including their culinary traditions—are blended.

Sausages are popular both in Germany and Denmark, and in South Jutland there is a regional dish called *kålpølser* (cabbage sausages), pork sausages served with creamed kale. Christiansfeld, a beautifully preserved 18th-century town founded by the Moravians, is famous for its *honningkager* (honey cakes). These heart-shaped spice cookies, baked using a secret recipe from 1783, are related to the German cookies known as *lebkuchen*.

The concept of a *kaffebord* (literally, "coffee table"), an overflowing buffet of treats, is of special significance in South Jutland. It originally provided an opportunity for the Danish-speaking minority in the territories annexed by the Germans from 1864–1920 to socialize, and became a point of pride for residents of the area. According to tradition, there must be at least 14 different types of cake—including 7 "soft" cakes (layer cakes and rolls), and 7 "hard" cakes (cookies). Any fewer can lead to comments by the guests that it is too bad that the hostess was too busy to do much baking. One of the traditional *kaffebord* cookies is called *gode råd* ("good advice"). It was said that women should always have these on hand for when friends came over for coffee and asked for "good advice" about this and that.

Another *kaffebord* specialty is the *rugbrødslagkage*, or *brødtærte*. This rye bread cake is made of small pieces of *rugbrød* mixed with eggs, sugar, and hazelnuts or almonds, with whipped cream and jam between the layers.

Vinsuppe, or wine soup, is a South Jutland specialty from the area around Tønder, a small city known for its handmade lace. Wine soup is made of whole barley groats, with prunes, raisins, and a bit of red wine added. The dish was traditionally served together with salty ham at christenings, funerals, and weddings.

Another specialty specific to South Jutland is the *solæg*, or sun egg. This ritual, which dates back to medieval times, requires aquavit and pickled hardboiled eggs. The ceremony is called to order by the blowing a special horn. Each guest is given a plate with an egg that has been boiled twenty minutes so that the yolk has turned dark blue and then halved, with the entire yolk on one half. After a toast regarding the significance of the sun and the symbolism of the egg, everyone removes the yolk, puts in a special spicy dressing that includes vinegar and mustard, and then puts the yolk back. The assembled company then raises their eggs simultaneously, says, "*Skål!*" before eating the egg, and then washes it down with a shot of *snaps*.

Central Jutland includes the long, windswept western coast. This area is abundant in seafood, and many different types of fish are available freshly caught from the North Sea. Local lamb and beef are also often on the menu.

Sea-buckthorn (*Hippophae rhamnoides*), which is called *havtorn* in Danish, grows along the dunes on the coast of Central Jutland. It was one of the first plants to grown in Denmark after the ice receded following the Ice Age, and is currently experiencing a renaissance thanks to the emphasis on foraging that is part of the New Nordic Cuisine movement. The slightly acidic berries of this bush are high in vitamin C and can be used as a flavoring for *snaps,* syrups, desserts, jam, and other dishes.

The island of Fanø, located off the west coast of Jutland near the port city of Esbjerg, is known for several specialties. One is a special version of the open-faced sandwich called *Fanø smørrebrød*. Different toppings are put on thin slices of white bread, which are then cut into wedge shapes and arranged on a plate as a round "cake" that looks a bit like a colorful pie chart. *Kaffepunch* (spiked coffee) is traditionally served with this *smørrebrød*. One recipe for *kaffepunch* says to put a coin in the bottom of a coffee cup, and then pour in enough coffee to cover it up. *Snaps* is then added until the drink is thin enough to reveal the coin hidden in the bottom.

Fanø's cuisine is strongly influenced by other cultures due to its seafaring tradition. It is thought that a local specialty called *sakkuk* originated in Holland. This dish is a boiled barley pudding topped with dark syrup, served with two or three types of boiled meat, sautéed salted pork cubes, potatoes, melted fat, and mustard.

Bakskuld is a fish specialty from Fanø that is also available in the Esbjerg area. It is made of salted, dried, and smoked *ising,* a flatfish known in English as a common dab (*Limanda limanda*). The fish fillet is fried and served hot on *rugbrød* together with *remoulade* sauce.

North Jutland, known as the "top of Denmark," is where the Skagerak and Kattegat meet. It is there that the Limfjord, which is no longer really a fjord, separates the islands of Vendsyssel-Thy and Mors from the rest of the Jutland peninsula. The tip of Jutland is known as Skagen, an area home to an important Danish art colony in the late 1800s.

Mors, which is the largest island in the Limfjord, is considered the oyster capital of Denmark. The primary source of income on this island, with its soft moraine hills and remnants of wild moors, has traditionally been agriculture and fishing. Today the concentration is on the fjord fishing of oysters and mussels.

The town of Hvide Sande, located on the narrow strip of land between the North Sea and Ringkøbing Fjord, is known for *tørrede dabs* or *ising,* which are smoked and dried common dabs. It is a common sight to see row after row of these flat fish hung up to dry like laundry behind the private homes in the area. Although the drying of fish originated as a method of preserving it, today dried dabs are promoted as the "sushi of Hvide Sande."

Just as wine-lovers enjoy touring vineyards, those who love aquavit enjoy touring the Snaps Route in North Jutland. One of the highlights of the trip is a visit to the city of Aalborg, which is considered the birthplace of *snaps* (sometimes referred to by the German spelling, *schnapps*). *Snaps* is also known as *akvavit* (aquavit, "the water of life"), and is distilled from either grain or potatoes. This strong alcoholic beverage has a distinctive taste that comes from dill and/or caraway seeds.

Some Danes like to create their own original *kryddersnaps* (spiced *snaps*) by adding herbs, berries, and other flavorings. *Bjesk* is a special term for *kryddersnaps* that is slightly bitter (the word *bjesk* is a regional version of *besk*, which means "bitter"), because it is flavored with an extract of *malurt* (wormwood).

Læsø is a large island off the northeast coast of the Jutland peninsula that was once thought to be the feasting ground of the Norse gods. Due to the high concentration of salt in its groundwater, it became known for its *sydesalt* (literally, "simmered sea salt") in the Middle Ages. Recently the salt industry has been revived, and salt is distilled from seawater the old-fashioned way, by evaporating it in handmade open iron pans over smoky fires built of the island's own wood. Læsø is also known for its *jomfruhummer* (small Norwegian lobsters) and smoked *fjæsing* (weever fish).

Aalborg has been making premium aquavit, also known as *snaps,* on the Jutland peninsula for over 150 years. Photo courtesy of Aalborg Akvavit and the Patchwork Group.

The Island of Bornholm

Bornholm is a beautiful 227-square-mile island located far from the rest of Denmark: south of Sweden, north of Poland, and some 97 miles east of Copenhagen. It has been a well-established trading post since the Viking era. During the Middle Ages, all of Western Europe was Catholic. Because Catholics were not allowed to eat meat on Fridays or during Lent, the demand for fish—especially preserved fish—was strong. Herring became a lucrative export for Bornholm—as well as for Zealand and the southern part of Sweden. Recently its fishing industry has suffered a sharp decline due to fish scarcity combined with low market prices arising from stiff competition. However there are still many restaurants along the coast that serve the catch of the day, which might include cod, salmon, and sole, in addition to various types of herring. The island is especially known for its smoked herring (most of which is now brought to Bornholm from elsewhere to be smoked) as well as other types of smoked fish. Visitors are always welcome at the old-fashioned *røgerier* (smokehouses), with their characteristic triangular chimneys, in seaside towns such as Arnager, Gudhjem, and Snogebæk.

One of Bornholm's signature dishes is a *smørrebrød* of smoked herring with the lyrical name *Sol over Gudhjem*, or Sun over Gudhjem. Gudhjem is a small, picturesque fishing village on the northeastern side of the island, and its name means "the Home of God." *Sol over Gudhjem* is an open-faced sandwich

Bornholm smokehouses were built to process local herring. At one time over 100 of these buildings, with their characteristic white chimneys, dotted the island. Photo courtesy of Røgeriet i Svaneke (The Svaneke Smokehouse).

made of smoked herring on *rugbrød*, topped with chives and a raw egg yolk representing the sun.

Residents of the island pride themselves on their *sildebord* (herring table). Similar to a *smørgåsbord*, the Bornholm *sildebord* features mostly fish dishes, including a variety of marinated and smoked herring. Of course, "the fish has to swim," as the saying goes, and therefore good quantities of *snaps* and beer are necessary. Another Bornholm specialty is an *ålegilde*, a party involving lots of eel.

In addition to its seafood, Bornholm has recently become known for dairy specialties, include Svaneke ice cream, made from the milk of the island's Jersey cows and its fresh fruits and berries. There are a number of local cheese specialties including a prize-winning Danablu from the prestigious St. Clemens Cheese Cooperative, made from the milk of cows that graze in the fields all summer. It is thought that the salt wind from the sea contributes to the taste of this special cheese.

In 1924 the bakery Johannes Dam & Søn created *rugkiks*, a classic Bornholm rye cracker, made up of 27 extremely thin layers of dough. Their light seasoning of caraway gives them a flavor that goes well with either cheese or jam. Jesper Dam is now the fifth generation carrying on this labor-intensive tradition of making crisp *rugkiks*.

Bornholm agricultural products that are exported to the rest of Denmark are highly respected, especially its poultry and cold-pressed rapeseed oil. Other specialties include beef and pork, flour, honey *snaps*, beer, licorice, chocolates, mustard, and jam.

Danish Holiday Traditions

The ethnically Scandinavian population of Denmark is overwhelmingly Lutheran, which might lead one to assume that they are active participants in the state-supported national Church of Denmark. However, less than 5% of church members attend Sunday services outside of holidays and special occasions. But the Danes love celebrations! The main holidays of the Christian calendar—plus one that is uniquely Danish—have their own special traditions, and in many cases also special foods. The special Danish holiday, *Store Bededag* (literally, "Great Prayer Day"), was established in 1686 to combine several minor prayer days into one day. Although there is talk from time to time about discontinuing *Store Bededag* as a paid holiday, it has remained on the calendar for over three hundred years.

Danes especially love Christmas. Instead of confining the celebration to Christmas Eve and Christmas Day, they add on Little Christmas Eve, Second Christmas Day, and sometimes even a day beyond that. Preparations for Christmas start weeks before the big day, including the debut in November of *julebryg*, a special sweet Christmas brew. This beer is intended to be enjoyed throughout the holiday season, and is served at Christmas dinner along with *snaps* and *gløgg* (hot mulled wine; see recipe, p. 43). Its debut on the first Friday in November (known as *J-Dag*) is a cause for celebration in itself.

Julefrokost (Christmas lunch) parties for friends and coworkers start in late November and are sometimes scheduled into January. These events are usually held in restaurants, and can extend through much of the afternoon and even into the evening. Restaurants are usually booked full during the day in the holiday season with parties for friends, coworkers, fellow union members, etc. The food at the *julefrokost* is often a *koldt bord* buffet with the addition of traditional Christmas foods such as roast pork, potatoes, red cabbage, and sometimes even *ris à l'amande* for dessert.

Danes have adapted the Swedish tradition of Santa Lucia Day as a school activity. A girl in each preschool or elementary school class is chosen to be St. Lucia. She is dressed in white, with a crown of candles, and together with a procession of her followers she brings around a tray of traditional saffron buns on the morning of December 13 to those in retirement homes, hospitals, and other institutions.

The baking of Christmas cookies gets an early start, and Denmark has many cookie traditions. *Klejner* are traditional Christmas cookies twisted into a knot before frying, and date back to the time when homes did not have ovens for baking. *Jødekager* (Jewish cookies) are cardamom Christmas cookies with a cinnamon-sugar-almond topping that probably take their name from the Jewish bakeries in Copenhagen. Other cookies that date back many centuries are *brune kager* (spiced round or rectangular "brown cookies"), *pebernødder* (spicy cookie balls), and *vaniljekranser* (vanilla cookies shaped like a wreath; see recipe, p. 67).

In addition to baking, many families make paper ornaments for the home and tree. Christmas trees are traditionally decorated with garlands of paper Danish flags, live candles, and a combination of homemade and heirloom ornaments that include woven paper hearts and *kræmmerhuse*, cornets filled with candy and cookies.

The day before Christmas Eve is called *lillejuleaften* (Little Christmas Eve), and is spent baking, shopping, decorating the tree, and wrapping gifts. Some families serve *risengrød*, warm rice porridge topped with cinnamon, brown sugar, and butter, on Little Christmas Eve. Leftovers of this porridge are often used for the rich *ris à l'amande* served as dessert at the Christmas Eve dinner. It is traditional to put out a bowl of rice porridge for the *nisser*, or elves, so that they won't cause any mischief.

Another traditional food for this day is *æbleskiver*, round, doughnut-like desserts made in a special pan (see recipe, p. 61). The name *æbleskiver* literally means "apple slices," because these national favorites originally contained pieces of apple, although today many different savory and sweet fillings are used. They date back to before the 1600s, when homes did not have ovens and desserts had to be made on the stovetop. *Æbleskiver* are made from a mixture similar to pancake batter, and must be manually turned during cooking in order to achieve a spherical shape. It is popular to serve *æbleskiver* with powdered sugar and jam, accompanied by *gløgg*.

Juleaften (Christmas Eve) is the main focus of the Christmas celebration. Families often attend church in the afternoon, and a big Christmas dinner then follows. This meal traditionally centers around a stuffed duck or goose, or roast pork with crackling—or in many homes, both poultry and pork. The entrée is served with boiled potatoes, caramelized potatoes, brown gravy, pickled red cabbage, and some kind of green cabbage. The various traditions around this side dish of green cabbage at Christmas are the subject of a surprising amount of local pride in Denmark.

Once the food of peasants and poor people, cabbage has long been a staple of the Danish diet. The "Amager Short-Stemmed" strain was introduced by the Dutch on Amager Island, south of Copenhagen, in the 15th century. The Dutch had been invited to settle in Denmark because of their advanced techniques in agriculture. (The fact that Crown Prince Christian II had fallen in love with a Dutch woman probably didn't hurt their cause.)

In most of Jutland at Christmas, *gammeldags hvidkål* (cabbage creamed with whipping cream and butter, called old-fashioned cabbage) is traditional. We would probably refer to *hvidkål* as being green, but the Danish name literally means "white cabbage" (referring to its white interior). Recipes for creamed cabbage vary throughout Jutland. In southern Jutland, the cabbage is first boiled and then chopped. It is allowed to dry, sometimes even until the next day, and then heavy cream is added. As one recipe says, "For God's sake, not milk!"

Danes in North Jutland, especially in the area known as Vendsyssel, enjoy a cabbage specialty called *grønlangkål* at Christmas (see recipe, p. 60).

Grønlangkål is a dish made of *grønkål* (literally, "green cabbage"), which in English is called kale. This very nutritious vegetable, with central leaves that do not form a head, was at one time one of the most common vegetables in Europe. It is well suited to the Danish climate because it can tolerate light frost and is rich is vitamin C, which can be in short supply in the Danish winter diet. In Denmark kale can be purchased fresh or already chopped into "balls." It is boiled, then pressed to remove all the liquid before being sautéed in butter or fat. Heavy cream (of course!) is then added. In Northern Jutland kale is eaten on Christmas Day with boiled bacon, *hamberger ryg* (smoked saddle of pork), ham, and/or sausage.

The island of Langeland lies southwest of Funen, and it too has a Christmas cabbage specialty. *Højkål* (literally, "high cabbage") is curly kale that is boiled and chopped before being browned in the fat from the pork roast, together with cubes of potato, to form a soft mixture served with the meat.

Dessert on Christmas Eve is traditionally *ris à l'amande* (also spelled *risalamande*), a creamy rice pudding with slivered almonds served with cherry sauce. A recipe for this traditional dessert is on page 64. A whole peeled almond is hidden in the pudding, and whoever finds it receives a small gift known as the *mandelgave* (almond gift)—sometimes a little marzipan pig. The gift of a marzipan pig is supposed to symbolize good luck and fortune in the year to come, a tradition that may have originated in Germany during a time that anyone owning a pig was considered to be very fortunate indeed.

After dinner the candles on the tree are lit, and traditionally this is the first time that children are allowed to see the decorated tree (although few modern families have a formal sitting room in which to hide it). The family sings Christmas carols while holding hands and "dancing" around the tree. A popular song says, "first the tree gets danced [around], and then it can be eaten," referring to the sweets tucked into the cone-shaped *kræmmerhuse* ornaments. Hot *gløgg* is sometimes served for the adults as everyone opens their gifts.

Christmas Day is usually spent paying visits to friends and family, often enjoying a lavish lunch that can extend into the early evening. Second Christmas Day (December 26) is for more visiting and eating, and also for relaxing. In fact many Danes have the entire week between Christmas and New Year off from school and work, and enjoy going for long walks after all the feasting.

The Danish celebration of *nytårsaften* (New Year's Eve) centers around watching the 6:00 PM broadcast of the queen's speech on television. There is

On Christmas Eve it is traditional to dance around the Christmas tree singing carols. Photograph courtesy of the Bengtsen/Jessen family.

a food tradition dating back to the 1700s of eating *nytårstorsk* (boiled cod with mustard sauce) on New Year's Eve, perhaps because this dish is less rich than most foods eaten during the Christmas season. In Southern Jutland creamed kale is associated with New Year's Eve, although both of these traditions are less common than they once were.

At midnight the striking of the clock on the Town Hall Square in Copenhagen is broadcast on television and radio, signaling that it is time for a champagne toast and *kransekage*. This marzipan ring cake, formerly popular as a wedding cake, is now a traditional New Year's Eve dessert throughout Denmark.

Those Danes who celebrate Mardi Gras with a *pinsekarneval* (carnival)—mostly those in Copenhagen—wisely do so in a warmer season than February (usually at the end of May). But there is a Danish tradition of celebrating the Sunday before Lent, called *Fastelavn*, that dates back as far as the holiday's name, which means "fast evening" or the day before Lent. *Fastelavn* is actually celebrated two days earlier, on Quinquagesima Sunday (the English name being a reference to the holiday being 50 days before Easter). Today children take turns hitting a modern representation of the traditional wooden barrel with a black cat in it to ward off evil. Instead of a cat, the barrel now contains candy and oranges, like a piñata, and the child who first breaks the barrel is crowned the cat queen. The child who breaks open the rest of the barrel is the cat king. Children dress in costume as on Halloween, an American holiday just beginning to be celebrated in Denmark.

Fastelavnboller are round sweet buns made specifically for this holiday. They are sometimes covered with icing, and are often filled, like a cream puff, with whipped cream that is either plain or flavored with chocolate or coffee. A traditional children's song for this holiday includes this verse: "*Fastelavn* is my name, and I want buns! If I don't get any, I'll cause mischief."

Påske (Easter) season in Denmark officially starts with the launching of a special beer for Easter called *påskebryg* on a Friday in early March. Like Danish Christmas beer, *påskebryg* (or *påskeøl*) features a seasonal label and a somewhat higher alcohol content than regular lagers. Since 1952 the launch day has been known as *P-Dag* (short for *Påskebryg Dag*). College students often gather to party on *P-Dag* in celebration of this special beer's debut, and pubs throughout Denmark host special *P-Dag* events.

Closer to Easter, children send a *gækkebrev* letter to friends or family members. The *gækkebrev* tradition dates back in the 18th century, when they included a flower called a *vintergæk*, or snowdrop (hence the name). The sender decorates the letter using paper cutting, perhaps adding a little poem, and revealing at most the first letter of his or her name and representing the number of the missing letters with pin pricks. The recipient has to guess who sent it. If the sender's name is not guessed correctly in a maximum of three attempts before Easter Day, he or she is owed an Easter egg. These eggs can be of any size or quality, but usually they are made of chocolate and wrapped in colorful foil paper.

In Southern Funen there is a special dish for the day before Good Friday, which is called *Skærtorsdag* (Maundy Thursday). *Skærtorsdagskål* (Maundy Thursday cabbage) is made by cooking several types of cabbage together with pork and other meats, and was once thought to have special power to prevent a type of malaria formerly found in areas of Denmark with brackish coastal water. Another version of this tradition, referred to as *syv slags grønt* (seven types of green), originally called for eating a soup made with nine kinds of fresh green vegetables (mostly cabbage!) on Maundy Thursday—but later this was often reduced to just seven kinds, especially since grass and nettles were sometimes needed to bring the total up to nine.

Danes in some parts of the country traditionally eat *skidne æg* the day before Easter. The name of this appetizer of eggs in mustard sauce literally means "shitty eggs." Legend is that because it was forbidden to clean the house or do laundry from Good Friday through Easter, this messy dish was appropriate for the time when clothes were not so clean. Today it is sometimes served on Maundy Thursday instead of on Holy Saturday.

The island of *Ærø*, south of Funen, has become known for its Holy Saturday egg boiling tradition that dates back more than a century. Local residents and tourists gather on the beaches to boil eggs in kettles of seawater while drinking beer and eating sausages grilled in the flames. They also eat *snobrød*, a favorite of Danes whenever they sit by a campfire. *Snobrød* is made by twisting white bread dough around a stick and toasting in like a marshmallow in the flames.

Easter Sunday is traditionally celebrated throughout Denmark with a lavish lunch. The table is festively set in spring colors, with chocolate eggs and flowers for decoration. The main course is often lamb or chicken, preceded by an appetizer featuring fish or eggs.

Anyone who has lived through a dark Scandinavian winter knows how precious the increased hours of daylight in the spring are. In Denmark spring unfolds itself gradually, and the Danes celebrate each new leaf. Home cooks and chefs eagerly make use of produce only available in the spring, including new potatoes, asparagus, rhubarb, and *ramsløg* (a type of wild garlic called ramsons in English). In fact the tiniest early potatoes sell for as much per kilo as a fine cut of meat, and are considered a real delicacy.

As mentioned, *Store Bededag* (Great Prayer Day) is celebrated on the fourth Friday after Easter as part of a whole series of work holidays in the spring. Although there is very little celebration associated with *Store Bededag*, there is a tradition of eating *varme hveder*, a type of warm, toasted wheat bun, the evening before. The tradition began when bakers, proscribed by law from opening their bakeries on *Store Bededag* itself, started making these buns the day before. It eventually became the custom to eat them fresh on Thursday evening instead of waiting until Friday.

Danes often meet with family and friends to have picnic dinner on *Sankt Hans Aften*. This June evening is the eve of the feast day of St. Hans (John the Baptist), and is also the night before the summer solstice. If the weather is good, everyone then proceeds to a large local bonfire, which is lit after dark and may be used to burn an effigy of a witch. This burning is supposed to send bad spirits in the form of the witch away to Bloksbjerg, a mountain in the Harz region of Germany where witches are said to congregate.

Mortensaften (Martinmas Eve) falls on November 10th, the eve of the Feast of St. Martin. Many Danes eat roast duck or goose on this evening. According to legend, the Roman monk Martin hid in a goose pen to modestly avoid being named a bishop. The cackling of the geese revealed his whereabouts, so it was therefore decided that every year on this day geese must lose their lives and be eaten. In actuality, November is a perfect time for a festive goose dinner, because it is a time in the late autumn when geese and other domestic animals are often slaughtered. Duck is now a common substitute because it is smaller and more readily available than goose.

Weddings, anniversaries, and birthdays call for festive social celebrations in Denmark. All rely heavily on the cheerful red and white Danish flag as decoration. In most restaurants you'll see a stash of "table flags" that can be borrowed to put on your table if you are celebrating a special occasion. And Danes have many special occasions, including birthdays (especially "round" ones such as 30, 40, 50, and 60), weddings, and special anniversaries (12½, 25, and 50). Although the traditions have changed somewhat with time, in the past these occasions called for a three-course meal made up of soup or a seafood appetizer, a main course centered around a roast of pork or beef, and then ice cream or mousse for dessert. Coffee would be served afterwards, with an after-dinner drink such as cognac, or a *hedvin* (fortified wine) such as brandy or sherry, and of course a piece of cake.

Most birthdays are celebrated with a *lagkage* (layer cake), often made with premade sponge-cake layers available in the grocery store. For a younger child's birthday there might be a *kagemand* or *kagekone* (cake man or cake woman) made out of puff pastry or *brunsviger* dough, the soft yeast dough that is a specialty of Funen. The cake is shaped like a man or woman and is decorated by the birthday child with icing and candy.

There was a time when the *kransekage* decorated with tiny national flags was the traditional wedding cake in Denmark, but today it is more common to see tiered cakes similar to those in the US. The layers are often dense tortes with jam, and marzipan is used to create a smooth exterior, decorative flowers, and other special touches.

Wedding dinners in Denmark are multi-course affairs with a special feature: songs written about the bride and groom, and sung by all the guests to well-known tunes. The words to the songs often rhyme and are written out on paper scrolls handed out to each guest at the table. There can be many speeches and toasts as well, so it is not unusual for a wedding or anniversary celebration to last for hours. Sometimes the party goes on so long that *natmad* (a midnight snack) is served before guests go home.

Tastes of Denmark

We are pleased to present an inviting array of Danish specialty dishes for you to try before your trip to Denmark, or to enjoy along with your happy memories after you return home. The recipes come from respected restaurant chefs, home cooks, cookbook authors, and online bloggers focusing on Danish cuisine. We appreciate them generously allowing us to share them with you, and are grateful to the many testers who helped us try out our new translations of the recipes we received in Danish.

All of the recipes have been adapted to American measurements and use ingredients mostly available in local grocery or specialty stores. Check *Resources* (p. 71) for sources of imported Danish foods and the special pans needed to make *rugbrød* and *æbleskiver*.

BEVERAGE

Glögg (Gløgg)

Hot mulled wine. Makes about 1 gallon.

Claus Meyer, co-founder of the famous Danish restaurant Noma, shares his recipe for this warm (and strong) alcoholic drink that is traditionally served at Christmastime. Meyer is considered the father of the New Nordic Cuisine movement.

> 1 HEAPING TABLESPOON WHOLE CLOVES
>
> 2 TABLESPOONS CARDAMOM SEEDS, COARSELY CRUSHED
>
> 2 STICKS CINNAMON
>
> ¼ OF A NUTMEG, COARSELY GRATED
>
> PEEL OF ONE ORANGE, PREFERABLY ORGANIC
>
> JUICE OF 3 ORANGES, PREFERABLY ORGANIC
>
> JUICE AND PEEL OF 1 LEMON, PREFERABLY ORGANIC
>
> 1 SMALL PIECE FRESH GINGER, CUT INTO 3 1-CENTIMETER CUBES
>
> 2 CUPS CANE SUGAR, PREFERABLY ORGANIC

[Glögg (Gløgg), *continued*]

⅓ CUP RAISINS, CHOPPED

4 TABLESPOONS BITTER ORANGE PEEL*

4 BAY LEAVES

2 TEASPOONS WHOLE BLACK PEPPER

1 TABLESPOON WHOLE ALLSPICE

4 0.75-LITER BOTTLES STRONG RED WINE

2 CUPS RED PORT

3 CUPS DARK RUM

1¼ CUPS DANISH *SNAPS* (AQUAVIT), PREFERABLY AALBORG BRØNDUMS†

RAISINS AND SLIVERED ALMONDS FOR GARNISH

Combine all the ingredients except the *snaps* and garnish in a stockpot with a tight-fitting lid. Heat to 210°F and simmer for an hour, keeping the *glögg* below a boil to retain the alcohol. Allow the *glögg* to steep at room temperature for 24 hours, then strain to remove the solids.

To serve, warm the *glögg* to 150–160°F and add the *snaps*. Serve immediately, topped with raisins and slivered almonds. (If you wish, you may soak the raisins in a little *snaps* an hour before serving.) For a sweeter *glögg*, add a bit more sugar.

*Use the peel of a fresh Seville orange or other type of bitter orange. Bitter orange peel also can be purchased dried in specialty shops such as those that sell home brewing supplies.

†Vodka may be substituted if *snaps* is not available.

APPETIZER

Gravad laks med rævesovs

Salted and marinated salmon with mustard sauce. Serves 8–10.

This recipe comes from Claus Christensen, a highly respected Danish chef and cookbook author. His intimate restaurant, Gammel Mønt, is housed in a building in the center of Copenhagen that dates back to 1732. *Gravad laks* literally means "buried salmon," and this method of preserving fish by curing it (originally by burying it in the sand) is centuries old. The salmon needs to be prepared more than a day in advance.

Marinated salmon

2¼ POUNDS SALMON FILLET (SKIN ON, PIN BONES REMOVED)

¾ CUP BROWN SUGAR

3 TABLESPOONS COARSE SALT

⅓ CUP FRESH GROUND BLACK PEPPER

⅓ CUP GROUND DILL SEEDS*

⅓ CUP GROUND FENNEL SEEDS*

⅓ CUP CHOPPED FRESH DILL, PLUS SPRIGS OF DILL FOR GARNISHING

Mustard sauce

1 CUP BROWN SUGAR

½ CUP WATER

SALT AND PEPPER TO TASTE

1 TABLESPOON WHITE WINE VINEGAR

1 CUP SMOOTH GREY POUPON DIJON MUSTARD (NOT WHOLE GRAIN)

Rub the flesh of the salmon with the marinade ingredients, in the order listed above. Place the fish skin-side down in a shallow non-metal dish and cover the dish tightly with plastic wrap. Allow to rest in the refrigerator for 36 hours.

To make the mustard sauce (*rævesovs*), boil the brown sugar and water, making sure the sugar is completely dissolved. Add the white wine vinegar and salt and pepper to taste. Cool to room temperature and whisk in the mustard until smooth. The sauce should be about the consistency of a vinaigrette salad dressing.

For a less spicy version, use a high-quality honey mustard (such as Koops') instead of Dijon and decrease the brown sugar to ½ cup.

Fully remove the rub from the salmon by patting it dry with a towel or rinsing and then patting dry. Cut the fish into thin slices and serve on white bread spread with a thick layer of cold butter. Top with lots of fresh dill and serve with mustard sauce.

*If you have a hard time finding pre-ground herbs you can grind your own using an herb grinder or a mortar and pestle.

BREAD

Rugbrød

Rye bread. Makes 2 large loaves or 3–4 small loaves.

This recipe comes from Marianne Busse, a Dane who lives in America. She has lived in the United States for fifteen years and found early on that she had no resource for traditional rye bread from a bakery as she would in Denmark. She came up with her own recipe with ingredients she could find locally. She always makes an extra loaf to freeze or share with friends!

This bread takes three days to prepare, so plan ahead. It is also best to bake the bread in special pans designed for making rye bread. Rye bread pans are deeper

[Rugbrød, *continued*]

and narrower than American bread pans, and can be hard to find. Pullman loaf pans (13″ × 4″ × 4″) without the lids may be used. If you use typical American loaf pans, butter the inside of the pan prior to filling with dough to facilitate removal.

Day one

1 OUNCE YEAST

½ CUP LUKEWARM WATER

½ CUP RYE FLOUR

Day two

6 CUPS LUKEWARM WATER

3 TABLESPOONS SALT

3 CUPS CRACKED RYE KERNELS (NOT WHOLE KERNELS!)

1½ CUPS RYE FLOUR

6 CUPS ALL-PURPOSE FLOUR

Day three

2 CUPS LUKEWARM WATER OR DARK BEER

10 CUPS RYE FLOUR

OIL FOR BRUSHING THE SURFACE OF THE DOUGH

On the first day, create a starter. Mix yeast, ½ cup lukewarm water, and ½ cup rye flour. Cover and let sit at room temperature for 24 hours. If you already have a starter (see below), remove it from the refrigerator and let it sit at room temperature for 24 hours.

On day two, stir 6 cups lukewarm water into the dough and add salt. Add cracked rye kernels, rye flour, and all-purpose flour. Cover with a dish towel and leave at room temperature for 12–24 hours. It will start to bubble, which means that the fermentation process is working!

On the third day, add 2 cups water or beer and additional rye flour. If the dough is not the consistency of wet oatmeal, add water ½ cup at a time until it is.

Put aside about 1 cup to use as a starter the next time you want to make rye bread. Sprinkle with salt and cover loosely. Store in the refrigerator for up to one month.

Pour the remaining dough into two large rye bread pans or three to four small ones. Make sure not to fill them up all the way, as the dough will rise. Cover with a dish towel and leave at room temperature for 4–6 hours.

Preheat the oven to 400°F. Pierce holes in the dough with a fork and brush the surface with oil. Bake for 2 hours at 400°F.

Remove the loaves from the pans, brush them with water, wrap in a dry dish towel, and put into a plastic bag upside down to steam as they cool. Cut into thin slices and top with your favorite *pålæg*!

Open-Faced Sandwiches

Dyrlægens Natmad

Veterinarian's midnight snack. Serves 1.

This is one of the best-known Danish *smørrebrød*, and one of the few with a special name. We enjoyed this dish at Orø Kro on the small island of Orø, which is located north of Copenhagen in the Isefjord and accessible by ferry from Holbæk.

Variations on this recipe include using butter rather than bacon fat, as well as the option of adding slices of crisp bacon. Garnishes could include fried crispy onions instead of raw onions, and sprigs of dill rather than watercress.

1 SLICE *RUGBRØD* (DANISH RYE BREAD)

BUTTER OR RENDERED BACON FAT

LEVERPOSTEJ (DANISH PORK LIVER PÂTÉ, SEE RECIPE, P. 49)

CORNED BEEF OR OTHER BRINED MEAT (*SALTKØD*) OR HAM

MEAT ASPIC (*SKY*), A GELATIN MADE FROM MEAT OR CHICKEN STOCK

Garnish

RAW RED ONION RINGS

PICKLED BEET SLICES

PICKLED CUCUMBER SLICES

WATERCRESS

Spread the bread with bacon fat (or butter). Add a layer of liver pâté, then slices of corned beef and a slice of aspic.

Top this open-faced sandwich with a garnish of red onion rings, a few pickled beet slices, pickled cucumber slices, and watercress. Eat with a knife and fork.

Karrysild

Curried herring. Serves 5–6.

This recipe also comes from Marcus Schioler, author of the Canadian *smørrebrød* blog www.danishsandwich.com. *Karrysild* is traditionally served on *rugbrød*, garnished with dill, chives, chopped raw onions, or hard-boiled egg.

5 PICKLED HERRING FILLETS, SLICED IN ½-INCH STRIPS

2 TABLESPOONS CRÈME FRAÎCHE*

2 TABLESPOONS MAYONNAISE

1 TABLESPOON DIJON MUSTARD

1 TABLESPOON MILD CURRY PASTE†

1 SHALLOT, THINLY SLICED

[Karryslid, *continued*]

> 1 DILL PICKLE, FINELY CHOPPED
>
> 1 TEASPOON CAPERS
>
> 1 TEASPOON PICKLED HERRING LIQUID
>
> ½ CRISP APPLE, CORED AND CHOPPED
>
> ¼ TEASPOON CRUSHED CORIANDER SEED
>
> ¼ TEASPOON CRUSHED MUSTARD SEED
>
> SALT AND PEPPER TO TASTE
>
> DILL, CHIVES, OR GREEN ONION FOR GARNISH

Stir to combine crème fraîche, mayonnaise, Dijon mustard, and curry paste. Add crushed spices, pickles, capers, onions, and pickling liquid and mix together. Refrigerate for least one hour to allow the flavors to mingle. Remove from the refrigerator and add the sliced herring and chopped apples to the sauce.

Serve about ⅓ of a cup of this mixture on a slice of buttered *rugbrød*, and garnish with dill and chives (or green onion). Eat with knife and fork.

*A mixture of 1 tablespoon sour cream and 1 tablespoon heavy cream is a good substitute.

†You may substitute 1 tablespoon curry powder and 1 tablespoon sour cream or crème fraîche. Mix well and allow time for the flavors to blend before adding the next ingredients.

Frikadeller

Meatballs of ground pork and veal. Serves 4.

Frikadeller are considered by many to be the ultimate Danish national dish, and they are served either at room temperature on an open-faced sandwich at lunch, or as a hot entrée with boiled potatoes and gravy for dinner. Marcus Schioler, author of the blog Danish Sandwich (www.danishsandwich.com), contributed his recipe for light-textured *frikadeller* with a hint of allspice. Marcus was born in Canada to a Danish father who instilled in him a deep passion for *smørrebrød*. Frustrated by the lack of Danish ingredients in local supermarkets, he focused his energies toward learning the secrets of preparing Danish open-faced sandwiches using ingredients available in North American supermarkets.

> ½ POUND OF FINELY GROUND PORK
>
> ½ POUND OF FINELY GROUND VEAL (BEEF MAY BE SUBSTITUTED)
>
> 1 MEDIUM ONION, GROUND ALONG WITH THE MEAT OR FINELY CHOPPED
>
> 1 LARGE EGG

1⅓ CUPS SODA WATER OR SELTZER

1 TEASPOON SALT

3 TABLESPOONS FLOUR (RYE OR WHEAT)

PINCH OR TWO OF GROUND ALLSPICE

FRESHLY GROUND PEPPER TO TASTE

BUTTER FOR PAN FRYING

Combine all the ingredients except the butter in a bowl. The mixture should be quite moist and soft, but you can add more flour if it seems too wet. Place a non-stick frying pan over medium-high heat and then melt a couple of tablespoons of butter in the frying pan. You will be frying the meatballs in batches.

Using a pair of spoons, form the meat mixture into a slightly flattened ball shape. Place these balls, one-by-one, in the hot frying pan. Don't put too many *frikadeller* in the pan at once—they should not be touching.

Cook the meatballs for about 3 minutes, and then flip gently. Cook for 3 minutes more and then remove them to a separate platter. Melt more butter in the pan and fry the next batch.

To enjoy *frikadeller* as a topping for *smørrebrød*, butter a piece of *rugbrød*, slather it with Dijon mustard, place a couple of sliced *frikadeller* on the mustard, and then top it with an appropriate garnish (for instance, *agurkesalat* or even dill pickles). Serve with a cold lager beer and eat with a knife and fork. You can also serve the *frikadeller* warm with boiled potatoes and brown gravy for dinner.

Leverpostej

Pork liver pâté. Makes two 4-cup loaves.

This recipe comes from Adam Aamann of the eponymous restaurant Aamanns in Copenhagen. He is often credited with revitalizing Denmark's *smørrebrød* tradition. *Leverpostej* is delicious on a piece of *rugbrød*, topped with bacon and sautéed mushrooms or with pickled beets; it is the foundation of traditional *smørrebrød* such as *Dyrlægens Natmad* (p. 47).

¾ POUND PORK FAT (YOU MAY NEED TO ASK A BUTCHER FOR THIS)

2 ONIONS, ONE CUT IN HALF AND THE SECOND IN QUARTERS

4 SPRIGS FRESH THYME, DIVIDED

4 FRESH BAY LEAVES, DIVIDED

1½ POUNDS PORK LIVER

4 ANCHOVY FILLETS

2 EGGS

[Leverpostej, *continued*]

> 3½ TABLESPOONS BUTTER
>
> ½ CUP FLOUR
>
> 4 CUPS WHOLE MILK
>
> 3 TABLESPOONS SALT
>
> 5 WHOLE ALLSPICE, GROUND WITH A MORTAR AND PESTLE
>
> FRESHLY GROUND BLACK PEPPER

Place the pork fat, one onion (cut in half), two sprigs of thyme, and two bay leaves in a pan with enough water to just cover the fat. Boil for approximately 30 minutes. Remove and discard the bay leaves and thyme. Run the cooked fat through a meat grinder twice (or chop carefully in a food processor). Process the second onion (cut in quarters) through the meat grinder along with the pork liver and anchovies. Then mix in the two eggs.

Make a roux by melting the butter in a saucepan, sprinkling the flour in gradually, and then adding the milk a little at a time while whisking thoroughly until the roux is smooth. Add salt, allspice, and pepper. Mix the roux into the chopped fat mixture and let this cool to about 85°F before stirring it into the liver. Mix thoroughly and add salt to taste.

Divide the pâté into two loaf pans and put the remaining bay leaves and sprigs of thyme on top. Place the loaf pans in a roasting pan filled with enough water to reach halfway up the sides, and bake at 375°F for 40 minutes.

Serve warm or at room temperature on *rugbrød* or the bread of your choice.

Stjerneskud

Shooting star open-faced sandwich. Serves 1.

This *smørrebrød*, with its inventive name, takes advantage of the varied seafood bounty available in Denmark. Chef Kasper Kallerup Hansen of Orø Kro on the tiny island of Orø allowed us to come into the kitchen to observe the construction of this impressive *smørrebrød*.

> 1 THIN SLICE FRENCH BREAD OR *RUGBRØD* (DANISH RYE BREAD)
>
> BUTTER
>
> 1 FRIED FILLET OF FISH, PREFERABLY PLAICE OR SOLE
>
> 1 FILLET OF PLAICE OR SOLE STEAMED IN WHITE WINE*
>
> 1 SLICE SMOKED OR CURED SALMON (OPTIONAL)
>
> 1–2 SPOONFULS LUMPFISH CAVIAR (USE RED AND BLACK FOR MORE COLOR)
>
> 2–3 SPOONFULS TINY BOILED SHRIMP, SHELLED

Garnish

LETTUCE

REMOULADE (P. 58), OR USE THE DRESSING BELOW

2 SPEARS STEAMED ASPARAGUS

DILL

LEMON TWIST

Dressing

1 TABLESPOON CRÈME FRAÎCHE

1 TABLESPOON MAYONNAISE

1 TABLESPOON WORCESTERSHIRE SAUCE

DASH TABASCO SAUCE

1 TABLESPOON KETCHUP

SALT AND PEPPER TO TASTE

Start assembling this *smørrebrød* by buttering the piece of bread, then adding an optional layer of lettuce. Next, place the room-temperature pieces of fried fish and steamed fish or herring. Then add salmon if you wish. The caviar and shrimp are on the top layer, together with a dollop of *remoulade* (p. 58) or dressing and a garnish of dill, asparagus, and a twist of lemon.
*Pickled herring may also be used.

SOUPS

Gule Ærter med Bacon
Winter pea soup with bacon or salt pork. Serves 10.
Camilla Plum is a Danish TV cooking celebrity and the author of over a dozen books on food and gardening. She lives on the organic farm Fuglebjerggård in Northern Zealand, where weekend visitors enjoy lunch, coffee, fresh baked goods, and fruit juices in the Cafe Palais de Poulet (located in the former henhouse). This version of the classic *gule ærter* soup comes from her book *The Scandinavian Kitchen*. As she says, "it is a dense, filling, and creamy winter soup. You can expand the concept by serving the soup with a plate of sausage or ham, and a batch of steamed vegetables."

2 CUPS DRIED SPLIT YELLOW OR GREEN PEAS

2¼ POUNDS MIXED VEGETABLES, SUCH AS CARROTS, CELERIAC, LEEKS,

AND PARSNIPS

6–8 CUPS WATER

[Gule Ærter med Bacon, *continued*]

2 CUPS VEGETABLE, PORK, OR CHICKEN STOCK, OR THE COOKING LIQUID

FROM A PIECE OF SALTED AND/OR SMOKED MEAT

7-OUNCE PIECE OF BACON OR SALT PORK

5 CLOVES GARLIC

1 SMALL BUNCH OF FRESH THYME

2 BAY LEAVES

1 SPRIG FRESH MARJORAM

¾ CUP CREAM (GENEROUS)

SCANT 1½ CUPS SHELLED FRESH OR FROZEN GREEN PEAS

2 TABLESPOONS BUTTER

SALT AND PEPPER

CHIVES TO GARNISH

Soak the dried peas in water for at least 8 hours, then drain. Rinse and peel the vegetables and cut into chunks.

In a large saucepan, simmer the dried peas in the water and stock with the vegetables, bacon, and herbs until tender. Remove the bacon, rinse it under cold water, and cut it into small dice, then fry in its own fat until golden and crispy. Purée the rest of the cooked ingredients in a food processor with the cream until smooth, and return to the pan.

Heat the fresh or frozen peas in the butter until very green. They must not cook, or they will turn brown. Purée until smooth in the food processor; then mix into the soup. If it is very thick, you can add some whole milk or more stock. Season with salt and pepper.

Serve with the crispy bacon and chives on top.

Viking Fiskesuppe

Viking fish soup. Serves 6–8.

This recipe from a thousand years ago comes to us courtesy of the Ribe VikingeCenter on the west coast of Jutland. Although the ingredient list specifies trout, the Vikings would sometimes have used cod, mackerel, or flat fish such as plaice, flounder, or dab. Fish and shellfish were an important source of protein for the Vikings, especially in coastal areas, and were either eaten fresh, or preserved by smoking, salting, or drying.

2 TABLESPOONS BUTTER

5 ONIONS, DICED

5 CARROTS, DICED

10 CUPS WATER

1 HANDFUL (ABOUT 1 CUP) CHOPPED CHERVIL*

1 HANDFUL (ABOUT 1 CUP) CHOPPED GARDEN CRESS

1 CUP FINELY CHOPPED SPRING ONION (SCALLION)

1 CUP HEAVY CREAM

2 POUNDS TROUT OR OTHER WHITEFISH, CUT INTO BITE-SIZED PIECES

SALT TO TASTE

Melt the butter in a large pot. Add the onions and carrots and sauté for 2–3 minutes. Add the water and bring to a boil. Leave to simmer until the vegetables are cooked al dente, then add the chervil, cress, spring onion, and cream. Add the fish to the soup. Simmer over low heat until the fish is cooked and tender, approximately 5 minutes. Season to taste with salt and serve with bread.
*Parsley may be substituted.

MAIN DISHES

Æggekage

Country omelet topped with crispy bacon. Serves 4–6.

This recipe is a specialty of Restaurant Carlslund in Odense. Chef Henning Engstrøm has owned the 150-year-old restaurant for the past 14 years. They serve this regional dish *ad libitum,* which means diners may have all they can eat.

5 PIECES LIGHTLY SALTED SMOKED DANISH PORK CRACKLING (RINDS)*

5 SLICES LIGHTLY SALTED SMOKED DANISH BACON (THICK-SLICED)

10 FRESH EGGS

1 CUP MILK

SALT AND PEPPER TO TASTE

1 TOMATO, THINLY SLICED INTO ROUNDS

2–3 TABLESPOONS CHOPPED CHIVES

Place pork rinds in a jelly-roll pan in an oven preheated to 325°F. Frequently pour off the fat. When there is no more fat, remove from the oven.
Fry the bacon in a pan on the stove until crispy. Make sure that the pan has a thick bottom and that it is large enough for the number of eggs you will be cooking. Remove the bacon and discard most of the bacon grease, retaining a small amount in the pan.

[Æggekage, *continued*]

Whisk the eggs, milk, salt, and pepper together in a bowl. Pour into the frying pan, preheated with a little of the bacon grease. Cook over medium heat, stirring the egg mass as little as possible while making sure it does not stick to the bottom. When the eggs are cooked almost all the way through, cover the pan, reduce the heat to low, and allow the eggs to rise. Ideally, the finished omelet will be between 1½ and 2 inches tall.

Leave the eggs in the pan. Lay the tomato slices on the top and sprinkle with chives. Top with pork rinds and bacon. Serve in the pan with rye bread and mustard on the side.

*This cut of pork can be extremely hard to find outside of Denmark. If you can't find it, double the amount of bacon used.

Skipperlabskovs

Sailors' beef stew. Serves 4–6.

This recipe, a traditional sailors' dish, comes from Grøften, one of Tivoli's oldest and most revered restaurants. Grøften has been in business at the famous Copenhagen historic amusement park since 1874, and according to owner Poul Eriksen, *skipperlabskovs* has long been one of their signature dishes. This is the Danish version of *scouse* or *lobscouse*, a hash-like stew popular throughout Northern Europe and Great Britain.

> 1 POUND WELL-TRIMMED STEWING BEEF, CUT INTO ¾-INCH CUBES
>
> 1¼ CUPS BEEF STOCK OR BOUILLON (OR WATER)
>
> 1 LARGE ONION, CHOPPED
>
> 3–4 BAY LEAVES
>
> 15 WHITE PEPPERCORNS
>
> 2¼ POUNDS POTATOES, PEELED AND SLICED
>
> SALT TO TASTE
>
> CHIVES FOR GARNISH
>
> PICKLED BEETS

Blanch the beef cubes in stock, bouillon, or water. Add the onion, bay leaves, and peppercorns, and boil for an hour, adding more liquid as necessary to keep the ingredients covered.

Add the potatoes and boil for an additional hour. Discard the bay leaves. Mash the potatoes and meat lightly with a whisk, blend well, and salt to taste. The consistency should be like porridge. If it is too firm, add a bit more liquid.

Serve with a generous amount of chopped chives on top and with a dish of chopped pickled beets on the side.

Langtidsbraiseret Svineskank

Slow-braised shank of Danish pork. Serves 3.

This recipe comes from the former restaurant Den Skaldede Kok (The Bald Chef) in Tivoli. Carsten Olsen, the owner and namesake of this restaurant, now runs a catering business in Helsingør.

3 PORK SHANKS*

7 TABLESPOONS BUTTER, DIVIDED INTO TWO PORTIONS

1½ LARGE ONIONS, CHOPPED IN LARGE CUBES

3 OR 4 FAT CLOVES GARLIC, PEELED

1½ COOKING APPLES, CORED AND CUBED

1 LEEK CUT INTO ¾-INCH SLICES

1½ CUPS DARK BEER†

2 CUPS CHICKEN STOCK

¼ CUP APPLE CIDER VINEGAR

6 SPRIGS THYME

4 SPRIGS SAGE

SALT AND PEPPER

Brown the pork shanks in 3½ tablespoons butter in a large pan. Set them aside and brown the onion, garlic, apples, and leeks in the same pan. Return the pork shanks to the pan and add the beer and chicken stock. Add the thyme and sage, and season with salt and pepper.

Allow the shanks to simmer, covered, about 1 hour, turning them occasionally if they are not fully submerged. Once the pork has reached an internal temperature of 145°F, remove them, and reduce the stock in the pan by about half. Strain the stock, discard the solids, and whisk in 3½ tablespoons cold butter, making sure that it does not come to a boil after the butter has been added. Add salt and pepper to taste. The pork shank and sauce should be served on mashed potatoes, garnished with pearl onions.

*Bone-in country style ribs or pork shoulder may be substituted for pork shanks.
†A good Danish beer to use would be Jacobsen Brown Ale.

Bagt Torsk, Citron Hummersauce, og Rødbedetatar

Baked cod, lobster lemon sauce, and beet tartar. Serves 4.

This New Nordic version of baked cod comes from Restaurant Els in Copenhagen. When it opened in 1853, this restaurant was a coffee house that was a favorite haunt of well-known actors from the nearby Royal Theater—including the aspiring actor Hans Christian Andersen. The baked cod and beet tartar created by chef David Loehr

[Torsk, Citron Hummersauce, og Rødbedetatar, *continued*]

for Restaurant Els are accompanied by a cold, siphoned potato purée, but are excellent when served with old-fashioned boiled potatoes as an alternative.

> 2 COD FILLET PORTIONS
>
> SEA SALT
>
> *Lobster lemon sauce*
>
> 2 CUPS CREAM
>
> ½ CUP LOBSTER STOCK*
>
> 1 SHALLOT, FINELY CHOPPED
>
> ½ LEMON, JUICE AND ZEST
>
> FRESHLY CHOPPED CHIVES (GARNISH)
>
> *Beet tartar*
>
> 1 POUND FRESH BEETS
>
> ½ ONION, FINELY CHOPPED
>
> 1 GRATED APPLE
>
> SMALL AMOUNTS OF OLIVE OIL, DIJON MUSTARD, CIDER VINEGAR,
>
> SHREDDED HORSERADISH, SALT, AND PEPPER

Prepare the beet tartar in advance. Cook the beets in boiling water until tender. Blanch, peel, and chop beets into small pieces. Fold in the chopped onion and apples. Season to taste with the olive oil, Dijon mustard, cider vinegar, shredded horseradish, salt, and pepper.

For the lobster lemon sauce, cook the lobster stock and lemon juice with the shallot until boiling, and then skim off and discard the shallot pieces. Add the cream. Reduce the sauce to the consistency of thick cream, then add the lemon zest and season with salt and pepper.

Close to the time you plan to serve the dish, preheat the oven to 350°F. Bake the cod on a buttered sheet pan for 18 minutes or until cooked through. Pull off the skin after baking and season with sea salt.

Plate the individual pieces of cod, pour sauce over the fish, and garnish with chives. Mold or pile the beet tartar neatly next to the fish, and serve with potatoes.

*Seafood stock may be substituted.

Gammeldags Kylling

Old-fashioned chicken with gravy. Serves 4.

This classic dish comes from Brdr. Price restaurant in Tivoli, owned by the famous celebrity chef Price brothers. It is always on the menu to offer visitors the chance to try this classic dish, but is traditionally enjoyed in the spring.

1 WHOLE ROASTING CHICKEN

SALT AND PEPPER

1 BUNCH CURLY-LEAF PARSLEY

3 TABLESPOONS BUTTER

1 CUP STRONG CHICKEN BOUILLON

2 CUPS CREAM

Season the inside of the chicken with salt and pepper and stuff it with parsley. Melt the butter in a cast-iron Dutch oven and when it has clarified, brown the chicken on all sides, using a wooden spoon to turn the chicken to avoid piercing the skin. When the chicken is nicely browned, add up to a cup of good chicken bouillon, reduce the heat, and cover. Allow the chicken to simmer about 30 minutes. Add the cream and continue to cook for approximately 15–20 more minutes until it is fully cooked. Remove the chicken and keep it warm.

Season the gravy left in the pot to taste. Do not thicken the gravy, as it is supposed to be separated. Serve with *agurkesalat* (cucumber salad, below), *rabarbarkompot* (rhubarb compote, p. 59), and boiled new potatoes.

CONDIMENTS & SIDE DISHES

Agurkesalat

Sweet and sour marinated cucumber salad. Serves 4.

A refreshing, crunchy, cucumber salad traditionally accompanies many dishes in Denmark, including pork and poultry entrées and *smørrebrød*. This recipe, which should be prepared a few hours or a full day before serving, comes from the Brdr. Price Restaurant in Tivoli and is delicious when served with their old-fashioned chicken (*gammeldags kylling*, p. 56).

2 ENGLISH-STYLE (BURPLESS) CUCUMBERS

½ TABLESPOON DRIED WHOLE CORIANDER SEEDS

2 OR 3 CLOVES

2 BAY LEAVES

1 TABLESPOON WHOLE BLACK PEPPERCORNS

1⅛ CUPS WHITE VINEGAR

1 CUP WATER

SUGAR AND SALT TO TASTE

Slice the cucumbers into thin slices using a mandolin or the side of a grater. Draw the moisture out of the cucumbers by sprinkling them with salt and letting them sit

[Agurkesalat, *continued*]

for an hour. Squeeze out as much moisture as possible and rub off any remaining salt. Place the cucumber slices in a bowl and set aside.

Put all of the spices except the salt and sugar into a small cheesecloth bag, and place the bag into a small saucepan with the vinegar and water. Bring the mixture to a boil, then turn off the heat and let it sit.

When this brining solution has cooled, discard the pouch of spices, and season the liquid with sugar and salt. Pour onto the cucumber slices. Cover and allow to marinate in the refrigerator for at least a couple of hours, but preferably overnight. Drain or serve with a slotted spoon.

Remoulade

Remoulade. Makes about 2 cups.

Remoulade originated in France, and many countries have their own version. In Denmark *remoulade* is a popular condiment used on *smørrebrød* to top roast beef or a fish fillet, and also is served as a type of tartar sauce with fried fish. This recipe comes from popular *smørrebrød* restaurant Aamanns in Copenhagen.

> *Vegetable mixture*

¼ POUND PEELED CARROTS

⅓ POUND PEELED PARSNIPS AND/OR CELERIAC

¼ POUND PEELED ONIONS

⅓ POUND CAULIFLOWER OR CHOPPED BOK CHOY

2–3 TEASPOONS SALT

> *Pickling liquid*

1 CUP VINEGAR

¾ CUP SUGAR

½ OF A FRESH CHILE PEPPER, CHOPPED (ABOUT ONE SPOONFUL)

½ TABLESPOON PAPRIKA

½ TABLESPOON MUSTARD SEEDS

½ TABLESPOON TURMERIC

½ TABLESPOON CURRY POWDER

1 TABLESPOON MUSTARD POWDER

> *Sauce*

1 TABLESPOON CORNSTARCH, MIXED WITH WATER

COARSE-GRAIN MUSTARD TO TASTE (OPTIONAL)

MAYONNAISE, APPROXIMATELY 1 CUP

Chop or slice the peeled root vegetables into 1-centimeter cubes. Divide the cauliflower into small florets and mix with the root vegetables in a bowl. Sprinkle with a few teaspoons of salt and refrigerate for a few hours or overnight.
Combine all ingredients for the pickling liquid in a large pot and bring to a boil.
Rinse the salted vegetables in cold water, drain, and cook in the pickling liquid for 15–20 minutes, until cooked but still crispy.
Strain and set aside the cooked vegetables, retaining and continuing to cook the liquid until it has reduced by one-third. Chop the cooled pickled vegetables finely. Stir the cornstarch into a little cold water, and whisk in a little at a time to thicken the pickling liquid.
Mix the liquid with the vegetables, cool slightly, and perhaps season to taste with a little coarse-grain mustard.
Measure the cooled pickles and mix in a bowl with an equal amount of mayonnaise. Season with salt if needed.

Rabarberkompot

Rhubarb compote. Serves 4.

Rhubarb compote is a popular accompaniment to any chicken or pork entrée during the short rhubarb season. This recipe, which comes from the Brdr. Price Restaurant in Tivoli, works best with a red variety, but can be made with any type of rhubarb.

1 BUNCH WINE RHUBARB (ABOUT 5 STALKS), CHOPPED INTO SMALL PIECES

1 CUP SUGAR

½ CUP LEMON JUICE

Place rhubarb in a saucepan with a little water. Add the sugar and lemon juice and bring slowly to a boil. When the rhubarb has just reached the point at which it becomes tender, remove from heat and cool to room temperature.

Rødkål

Pickled red cabbage. Makes about 4 cups.

Pickled red cabbage is very popular in Denmark, served with pork or *frikadeller* either cold as a garnish on *smørrebrød*, or warm as a side dish at dinner. It is sometimes prepared using *ribssaft* or *ribsgele* (red currant juice or jelly) or *æblemost* (apple juice). This recipe, which features apple slices, is from the Danish-Canadian Marcus Schioler, author of the *smørrebrød* blog www.danishsandwich.com.

1 MEDIUM HEAD RED CABBAGE

1 SMALL WHITE ONION

3 TABLESPOONS BUTTER

[Rødkål, *continued*]

>3 TABLESPOONS SUGAR
>
>3 TABLESPOONS WHITE OR CIDER VINEGAR
>
>PINCH OF THYME
>
>2 BAY LEAVES
>
>¼ CUP WATER
>
>4 APPLES (GRANNY SMITH ARE BEST), CORED, PEELED, AND SLICED THINLY
>
>SALT AND PEPPER TO TASTE

Remove and discard outer leaves of cabbage, then cut cabbage into quarters and remove the white core. Thinly slice the cabbage with a chef's knife across the quarters widthwise. Peel and thinly slice the onion.

Melt the butter over medium heat in a large Dutch oven. Mix in the sugar.Add the cabbage and onion and stir to coat with butter. Add water, vinegar, thyme, and bay leaves. Heat to a boil, cover, and then simmer for 30 minutes. Add apples to the cabbage, plus a little salt and pepper.

Continue simmering for about 1 hour, stirring occasionally and adding a bit of water as necessary. The cabbage shouldn't be allowed to get too dry; there should always be a bit of liquid at the bottom of the pot. When done, the apples should be the consistency of purée and the cabbage tender. Generally, the taste of *rødkål* is even better the day after cooking.

Grønlangkål

Creamed kale. Serves 6.

This recipe comes from Camilla Plum's book *The Scandinavian Kitchen*. As she states in her book, "creamed kale is loved by everyone, if it's made properly. The name must be taken seriously and the cream must not be replaced with milk and flour, even if it may look the same. It is eaten with *frikadeller*, *medisterpølse* (sausage), smoked meats or ham, and is absolutely essential for Christmas lunch. It is usually served with caramelized potatoes—a very good match. The best creamed kale is made by boiling the leaves in some kind of stock, which need not be any more ambitious than the liquid from the meat you intend to eat with it; this is the method used here."

>1 WHOLE STEM OF KALE, OR ABOUT 2 POUNDS OF KALE LEAVES
>
>8 CUPS COOKING LIQUID FROM SALTED OR SMOKED MEAT
>
>½ TEASPOON GROUND MACE
>
>1 TABLESPOON COARSE SEA SALT
>
>1 TEASPOON COARSELY GROUND BLACK PEPPER
>
>1 TABLESPOON CORNSTARCH

1¾–2 CUPS HEAVY CREAM

3–5 TABLESPOONS SUGAR

Remove the coarse ribs from the kale leaves, then blanch in a large saucepan of boiling water until tender; about 5 minutes. Drain well in a large colander. Stack the leaves and chop them coarsely.

Place the chopped kale in a saucepan with the stock, mace, salt, and pepper (omit salt if the cooking liquid is very salty). Simmer uncovered, stirring frequently, until the kale is very soft. This may take as long as 45 minutes.

Strain, reserving the liquid, and return the kale to the pan. Mix the cornstarch with a little of the cream, then add to the pan along with the sugar and the rest of the cream, stirring vigorously. You may want to add some of the cooking liquid. Stir until the floury taste is gone. Adjust the seasoning and the creaminess, adding more cooking liquid if it is too dry. Eat the kale piping hot. It will keep in the refrigerator for 3–4 days.

DESSERTS

Æbleskiver

Round Danish doughnuts/pancakes. Makes 21 *æbleskiver.*

Æbleskiver are not really doughnuts or pancakes (although the mixture used to make them is similar to pancake batter). They're delicious spheres that can be served dusted with sugar or filled with jam or savory ingredients. Making *æbleskiver* requires a special stovetop pan, and it can take some practice to turn them correctly. Our recipe is used by permission from the book *Ebelskivers: Danish-style filled pancakes and other sweet and savory treats*, by Kevin Crafts. You will find recipes for many variations in his book, and numerous videos online to help you learn the trick to making perfectly round *æbleskiver*.

1 CUP ALL-PURPOSE FLOUR

1½ TEASPOONS SUGAR

½ TEASPOON BAKING POWDER

¼ TEASPOON SALT

2 LARGE EGGS, SEPARATED

1 CUP WHOLE MILK

3 TABLESPOONS UNSALTED BUTTER, MELTED AND COOLED SLIGHTLY

CONFECTIONERS' SUGAR, FOR DUSTING

Preheat the oven to 200°F. In a large bowl, whisk together the flour, sugar, baking powder, and salt. In a small bowl, lightly whisk the egg yolks, then whisk in the

[Æbleskiver, *continued*]
milk and 2 tablespoons of melted butter. Add the yolk mixture to the flour mixture and, using a wooden spoon, stir until well blended. The batter will be lumpy.
In a clean bowl, using an electric mixer on high speed, beat the egg whites until stiff, but not dry, peaks form. Using a silicone spatula, fold about one-third of the egg whites into the batter to lighten it, then fold in the rest just until no white streaks remain.
Brush the wells of an *æbleskiver* pan with some of the melted butter and place over medium heat. When the butter starts to bubble, add about 3 tablespoons of batter to each well. Cook until the bottoms of the *æbleskiver* are lightly browned and crisp, 3–5 minutes. Use 2 short wooden skewers to turn all of the *æbleskiver* and cook until lightly browned on the second side, about 3 minutes longer.
Transfer the finished *æbleskiver* to a platter and keep warm in the oven while you repeat to make two more batches. Dust the warm *æbleskiver* with the confectioners' sugar and serve right away.

Æblekage

Apple charlotte. Serves 2.
This recipe comes from the restaurant Søstrene Olsen in Hornbaek on the north coast of Sjælland, courtesy of Chef Thorleif Aagaard (who has owned the restaurant with his wife since 1982). Although the name means "apple cake," this unbaked dessert is actually closer to a pudding or trifle.

> 4 GRANNY SMITH APPLES, CORED AND SLICED
>
> SUGAR TO TASTE
>
> VANILLA TO TASTE
>
> *Egg cream*
>
> 1 EGG, DIVIDED
>
> 2 TABLESPOONS SUGAR
>
> ¼ CUP WHIPPING CREAM
>
> 1 TEASPOON FLOUR
>
> ZWIEBACK TOAST (OR OTHER PLAIN CRISP COOKIE) CRUMBS
>
> *Topping*
>
> CONFECTIONERS' SUGAR
>
> WHIPPED CREAM (IN DENMARK WHIPPED CREAM IS UNSWEETENED)
>
> SUGARED ALMOND SLIVERS

Preheat oven to 350°F. Put enough water in a small pan to cover the bottom. Sauté the apples until they are soft, adding sugar and vanilla to taste.

To make the egg cream, whip one egg yolk until nearly white, adding sugar. In a separate bowl, whip one egg white until completely stiff. In a third bowl, whip ¼ cup whipping cream with 1 teaspoon of flour. Fold the egg yolk, egg white, and whipped cream together carefully.

Coat the bottom and sides of a small baking dish such as a ramekin with butter and cookie or biscuit crumbs. Fill it halfway with the sautéed apples. Cover the apples with a layer of the egg cream mixture. Bake for 20 minutes. Allow to cool.

Dust with confectioners' sugar and serve at room temperature topped with whipped cream and sugared almond slivers.

Kærnemælkskoldskål

Buttermilk dessert. Serves 4–6.

This is a summer favorite in Denmark. The recipe comes from our good friend Annette (Bengtsen) Jessen, who became Carol's first Danish friend in a high school in New Jersey some 50 years ago.

2 PASTEURIZED EGG YOLKS*

2 TABLESPOONS SUGAR

1 TEASPOON VANILLA EXTRACT OR ½ VANILLA BEAN POD SEEDS†

4 CUPS (1 QUART) BUTTERMILK

½ LEMON

12–18 *KAMMERJUNKERE* (MAY SUBSTITUTE BUTTER-TOASTED OATS)††

Butter-toasted oat topping

2 TABLESPOONS BUTTER

2 TABLESPOONS SUGAR

¾ CUP OATS

Beat the egg yolks, sugar, and vanilla until they are airy. Add the buttermilk during the mixing. Add lemon juice to taste. Refrigerate until time to serve. Top with *kammerjunkere* or butter-toasted oats.

For the butter-toasted oat topping, let the butter melt in a pan over high heat, but without browning. Add the oats and sugar. Sauté this mixture at a high temperature while stirring for approximately 2 minutes. Turn down to medium heat and continue to cook, stirring constantly, about 5 minutes or until the oatmeal is light golden brown and crisp. Place a piece of wax paper on a wire rack. Spread the toasted oatmeal on parchment paper and allow to cool.

*Because the yolks will not be cooked, it is important that they be pasteurized.

†Split pod in half and scrape out seeds with a knife.

††*Kammerjunker* is a type of twice-baked biscuit or cookie available in Denmark. Any crunchy vanilla cookie, such as Nabisco Nilla Wafers, may be substituted.

Ris a l'Amande med Kirsebær Sovs

Rice pudding with cherry sauce. Serves 6–8.

The recipe for this rich Christmas dessert comes from the grandmother of Nete Schmidt, Distinguished Lecturer in Scandinavian Studies at the University of Wisconsin–Madison. She inherited her grandmother's handwritten cookbook and remembers her mother consulting it frequently. One whole, peeled almond is hidden in the pudding, and the lucky person who finds it is traditionally given a small gift such as a marzipan pig. The one who finds the almond is supposed to conceal the discovery as long as possible so that others will continue to look for it.

Note that the rice porridge needs to be made the day before the *ris a l'amande* is served on Christmas Eve—and both can be prepared two or three days earlier.

Rice porridge

½ GALLON WHOLE OR 2% MILK

1 CUP SHORT-GRAIN WHITE RICE OR *GRØDRIS**

2 TABLESPOONS SUGAR

2 TEASPOONS VANILLA SUGAR†

2 CUPS WHIPPING CREAM

ONE WHOLE ALMOND, BLANCHED AND PEELED

SLIVERED ALMONDS (OPTIONAL)

Cherry sauce

2 15-OUNCE CANS OREGON BING CHERRIES IN HEAVY SYRUP, OR FROZEN CHERRIES IN SUGAR

2 TABLESPOONS CORNSTARCH

CHERRY HEERING LIQUEUR OR KIRSCHWASSER TO TASTE (OPTIONAL)

To make the rice porridge, bring the milk to a boil while stirring, being careful not to burn it. Pour in the rice and stir until it all boils again. Cover and simmer for an hour at a low heat, stirring frequently so it doesn't burn. Remove the pot from the heat and add the sugar and vanilla sugar (add more sugar if you like it sweeter). Allow to cool, covered, and refrigerate overnight.

The next day, whip the cream and mix it into the rice porridge. If you will not be serving the *ris a l'amande* the same day, whip the cream slightly longer.

To make the cherry sauce, boil the cherries and syrup. Dissolve the cornstarch in a small amount of lukewarm water and add this mixture gradually to the cherries to thicken the sauce. Simmer one minute, then remove from heat to cool. Add cherry liqueur to taste if desired.

Serve the *ris a l'amande* cold or at room temperature. Add slivered almonds before serving, if desired, and put in one whole peeled almond for the almond prize.

*Special rice for making porridge.

TOP Cooking in an Iron Age kitchen at Museum Silkeborg, the Central Jutland museum renowned for its exhibit of the preserved remains of the early Iron Age Tollund Man. **MIDDLE LEFT** Viking bread baking began with flatbread made over an open fire and evolved to loaves baked in small ovens. **MIDDLE RIGHT** Simmering a kettle full of *Viking fiskesuppe* (fish soup). **BOTTOM** Preparing seafood at the Ribe VikingeCenter. Ribe is Denmark's oldest town, founded in 700 as a Viking marketplace.

TOP LEFT A kitchen maid prepares a stove-top dessert in one of the 75 historic buildings at Den Gamle By open-air museum in Aarhus. **TOP RIGHT** An antique *æbleskiver* pan at the National Museum of Denmark in Copenhagen. **MIDDLE LEFT** Baking *vaniljekranser* (vanilla wreath cookies) at Den Gamle By. **MIDDLE RIGHT** A *kræmmerhus* filled with little cookies hangs next to a marzipan pig on a historic Christmas tree. **BOTTOM LEFT** *Vaniljekranse* cookies. **BOTTOM RIGHT** Selling an array of historically accurate treats in the 1885 bakery at Den Gamle By.

TOP LEFT *Æbleskiver* dusted with sugar and served with jam.   **TOP RIGHT** *Rødgrød med fløde*, a popular berry pudding (and tongue-twister).   **MIDDLE LEFT** Six types of pastry from Lauras Bakery: clockwise from the top left: *grovsnegl* and *kanelsnegl* (both with chocolate), *thebirkes* (with poppy seeds), *hindbærsnitte* (raspberry bar), chocolate croissant, and in the center, *brunsviger*.   **MIDDLE RIGHT** *Kransekage*, an almond cake served on New Year's Eve.   **BOTTOM LEFT** A heavily laden traditional "Southern Jutland coffee table."   **BOTTOM RIGHT** Chef Thorleif Aagaard with his *æblekage* (apple charlotte).

TOP LEFT Chef Kasper Kallerup Hansen demonstrates the creation of a *stjerneskud* (shooting st... *smørrebrød* (open-faced sandwich). **TOP RIGHT** *Stjerneskud* at Orø Kro. **MIDDLE LEFT** *Sol over Gudhj...* (sun over Gudhjem), a traditional *smørrebrød* from Bornholm made with smoked herring and a r... egg yolk. **MIDDLE RIGHT** *Leverpostej* (liver pâté) *smørrebrød* with a garnish of bacon and mushroom... **BOTTOM** A few of the thirty different traditional *smørrebrød* available at Restaurant Kronb... in Copenhagen.

TOP LEFT Platter of *pålæg* (cold cuts and cheese) used to create your own *smørrebrød*. **TOP RIGHT** Two types of *rugbrød* for use as the base for *smørrebrød*. **MIDDLE** Three types of *smushi*, the Royal Cafe's combination of *smørrebrød* and sushi. **BOTTOM LEFT** *Smørrebrød* queen Ida Davidsen and her son Oscar Davidsen Siesbye, great-grandson of founder Oskar Davidsen. **BOTTOM RIGHT** *Smørrebrød* featuring Riberhus Esrom, a cheese that has received special designation by the EU stating it can only be produced in Denmark.

TOP LEFT Home cook Søren Jessen with the classic *stegt flæsk med persillesovs* (fried pork with potatoes parsley cream sauce). **TOP RIGHT** Restaurant Mellem Jyder, the oldest restaurant in Ebeltoft on the east coa of Jutland, dates to 1610. **MIDDLE LEFT** Christmas favorite *flæskesteg* (pork roast with crackling **MIDDLE RIGHT** *Frikadeller* (meatballs of pork and veal). **BOTTOM LEFT** Tiny *fjordrejer* (shrimp) at Grøfte the oldest restaurant in Tivoli. **BOTTOM RIGHT** Chef Henning Engstrøm at Restaurant Carlslund in Oden with his all-you-can-eat *æggekage* (country omelet with crispy bacon and fried pork rinds).

OP LEFT Carsten Olsen, known as The Bald Chef, with his *langtidsbraiseret svineskank* (slow-braised pork ank). **TOP RIGHT** Artistic plating of glazed beets with smoked ox-bone marrow, apples, and sorrel at oma, designated four times as Best Restaurant in the World. **MIDDLE LEFT** *Skipperlabskovs* (sailor's ew), a signature dish at Tivoli's Grøften restaurant. **MIDDLE RIGHT** New Nordic version of poached cod om Restaurant Els in Copenhagen. **BOTTOM LEFT** Danish "old-fashioned" chicken (*gammeldags kylling*) rved with cucumber salad, at the Bdr. Price Restaurant. **BOTTOM RIGHT** Claus Meyer, cofounder of oma and a leader in the New Nordic Cuisine movement.

TOP LEFT Cheesemonger on the shopping street in Ebeltoft. **TOP RIGHT** A traditional *gammeldags* (old-fashioned ice cream cone) complete with a *flødebol* (chocolate-covered cream cookie), jam, and *dr* (sprinkles). **MIDDLE LEFT** Hot dogs from a *pølsevogn*, served with the bread on the side. **MIDDLE RIGHT** Fresh rhubarb, a welcome sign of spring in Denmark. **BOTTOM LEFT** *Spegepølse* and other sausag at a market. **BOTTOM RIGHT** Danish radishes, used as a garnish on *smørrebrød*.

Mazarinkage

Almond cake. Serves 8–10.

This delicious almond cake recipe yields one 10-inch cake. For a chocolate version replace half of the flour with cocoa powder. The recipe comes from the Odense Marzipan Company on the island of Funen. Make sure that you use Odense Almond Paste rather than Odense Marzipan, which has a higher ratio of sugar to almonds and is used to make candy.

1 7-OUNCE BOX ODENSE ALMOND PASTE

½ CUP GRANULATED SUGAR

1 STICK (8 TABLESPOONS) BUTTER, AT ROOM TEMPERATURE

3 EGGS, AT ROOM TEMPERATURE

½ CUP CAKE FLOUR

CONFECTIONERS' SUGAR OR CHOCOLATE GANACHE (OPTIONAL)

Preheat oven to 350°F. Grease and flour a tart pan. Grate the almond paste using a cheese grater or box grater.

Add grated almond paste, sugar, and butter to a mixing bowl. With mixer on low speed, combine ingredients, then beat on high for 2–3 minutes. Add eggs, one at a time, beating well between each. Beat on high until batter is light-colored and fluffy (about 3 minutes more).

Sift cake flour into almond mixture. Gently fold in flour by turning with a spatula until ingredients are just incorporated. (Do not stir.)

Spread batter into a 10″ tart pan. Bake 30 minutes or until golden and a toothpick inserted in the middle comes out clean.

Let the cake cool completely on a wire rack before removing from pan. Sprinkle with confectioners' sugar or spread with chocolate ganache, if desired.

Rødgrød med Fløde

Red fruit pudding with cream. Serves 6–8.

This traditional dish isn't found on many restaurant menus, but you're likely to be served it if you are a guest in a Danish home during the summer season. If you're planning to go to Denmark you may want to practice pronouncing saying *rødgrød med fløde*—it's not easy! Our recipe comes from *Spise med Price*, a cookbook by the famous Price brothers James and Adam. In addition to being celebrity chefs and restaurant owners, James is a composer and conductor, and Adam is a screenwriter, whose credits include the popular TV political drama *Borgen*.

½ PINT STRAWBERRIES

½ PINT RASPBERRIES

[Rødgrød med Fløde, *continued*]

> ½ PINT RED CURRANTS
>
> ½ PINT BLACK CURRANTS*
>
> 1 CUP WATER
>
> 1¼ CUPS SUGAR, ADJUSTED TO TASTE
>
> 1½ TABLESPOONS POTATO STARCH (OPTIONAL)
>
> HEAVY CREAM, FOR GARNISH

Rinse, clean, and remove stems from the berries. Put them in a saucepan with the water and sugar. Bring slowly to a boil, skimming off the foam. Boil carefully for 3–4 minutes. If you wish to thicken the porridge, dissolve the potato flour in a little water and stir this into the berry mixture when it is just below the boiling point. Some people prefer to have large pieces of berry in their porridge. To do this, add the most fragile berries, such as the raspberries and the optional blackberries, at the last minute—ideally after the saucepan has been removed from the heat. Let the mixture stand so that these berries are warmed by the hot porridge. Adjust the quantity of sugar to the sweetness of the berries you are using.

Serve the cooled porridge with heavy cream at the highest fat content you can find.

*Other berries, such as blackberries, may be used.

Rababertrifli

Rhubarb trifle. Serves 4.

This dessert was a favorite of Kate Bengtsen, who opened her heart and home to our family, introducing us to many of the delights of Danish culture. It is shared here by her daughter Annette Jessen. The trifle can be made using fresh plums, pitted and chopped, if rhubarb is not in season. When made with plums, it is called *blommetrifli*.

> 1 POUND THIN RHUBARB STALKS, CUT INTO ½-INCH PIECES
>
> ½ CUP SUGAR
>
> 2 EGG YOLKS
>
> 3 TABLESPOONS SUGAR
>
> 1 TABLESPOON CORNSTARCH
>
> ½ CUP HEAVY CREAM
>
> 1 VANILLA BEAN POD, INCLUDING BEANS, CUT IN HALF LENGTHWISE*
>
> 6–8 LARGE ALMOND MACAROONS, CRUMBLED
>
> 2–3 TABLESPOONS SWEET SHERRY
>
> WHIPPED CREAM FOR DECORATION (UNSWEETENED)

Boil the rhubarb together with the sugar in a very small amount of water (a few tablespoons) until soft. Allow to cool.

Make the custard by whipping the egg yolks together with the sugar and then adding the cornstarch. In a saucepan, bring the heavy cream to a boil together with the whole split vanilla bean pod or vanilla extract. Pour the hot cream into the egg yolk mixture while stirring constantly. Return the entire mixture to the saucepan and heat, stirring constantly, until close to the boiling point. This mixture must not boil, because that may cause it to separate. Remove the pan of custard from the heat and allow it to cool. Discard the vanilla bean pod.

Divide the crushed macaroons in the bottom of a serving bowl, or in individual bowls, and drizzle them with the sherry. Add the rhubarb mixture, followed by the custard. Top with unsweetened whipped cream for decoration.

*Two teaspoons vanilla extract may be substituted.

†Use Amaretti or other Italian style such as biscotti.

‡Brandy or another type of liquid can be used to moisten the macaroons.

Vaniljekranser

Vanilla ring cookies. Makes approximately 80 cookies.

These traditional Christmas cookies date back to 1866. This old-fashioned version comes from the open-air historical museum Den Gamle By (The Old Town) in Aarhus. If you visit, you can go to the bakery and taste these cookies, as well as many other tasty treats from the past!

> 4¼ CUPS FLOUR
>
> 1 EGG
>
> 1 CUP PLUS 2 TABLESPOONS BUTTER
>
> 1¼ CUPS SUGAR
>
> ½ POD VANILLA BEAN, FINELY CHOPPED INCLUDING SEEDS*
>
> 1¾ CUPS CHOPPED ALMONDS

Preheat oven to 350°F.

Knead the flour, egg, butter, sugar, vanilla, and almonds together until the dough comes off your hands. Form the dough into a long sausage. If the dough is too dry, add water as necessary. Slice off small pieces and roll them on the counter into 4-inch strips. Join the ends of each strip to form a ring, making sure that there is a hole in the center large enough that the dough won't fill in during baking. Use some extra flour on your fingers to keep the dough from sticking.

If you want ridges on the cookies, chill the dough and use a cookie press or meat grinder with a special plate, or a piping bag with a star decorating tip, to create this texture before forming the rings by hand.

Bake 15–20 minutes at 350°F until light brown.

*You may substitute 1 teaspoon of vanilla extract; the cookies will be smoother.

Citronfromage

Lemon mousse. Serves approximately 8.

This recipe comes from chef Rasmus Kristensen of The Copenhagen, a restaurant in New York City specializing in Danish cuisine including lunch *smørrebrød* and authentic dinner entrées. Although the name *citronfromage* means "lemon cheese" in French, the Danish version is a rich, creamy dessert.

3 SHEETS GELATIN

4 LARGE PASTEURIZED EGG YOLKS

⅓ CUP SUGAR

⅓ CUP LEMON JUICE

ZEST OF 1 LEMON

1 VANILLA BEAN

1 PINCH SALT

2¼ CUPS WHIPPING CREAM

Soak the gelatin in ice water.

Whip the egg yolks with sugar, vanilla, and salt until aerated (this adds volume to the egg yolks and makes the mixture lighter in color).

Heat the lemon juice and zest in a small pot. Dissolve the gelatin into the hot juice.

Whip the cream to soft peaks.

Pour the lemon juice with gelatin into the egg yolk mixture. Mix with a whisk. Fold in the whipped cream.

Allow the mousse to set for at least 3 hours in the refrigerator before serving.

Shopping in Denmark's Food Markets

Helpful Tips

Outdoor Markets

Denmark's climate does not make year-round outdoor markets practical, although often there will be a fresh fruit or honey vendor on the *gågade* (walking street). Danes have a great love of pedestrian malls, and most larger cities feature at least one street designated as a *gågade* for shopping and dining.

Outdoor markets are often held once a week in season on or near the walking street, traditionally in the market square (*torv*). It is worth noting that Danes do not usually negotiate about price, although vendors are usually willing to sell you whatever quantity you desire and to provide information about their products.

As part of the New Nordic Food Cuisine movement, Copenhagen has created a new Torvehallerne market on the site of the city's market square. This year-round facility includes both indoor and outdoor vendors, and is a great place for visitors to explore the wide range of Danish produce, fish, cheese, meats, preserves, and even wine and beer. There are a number of restaurant stalls in the two halls, and outdoor vendors feature vegetables and fruits from around the country during the growing season.

Grocery Stores and Specialty Shops

Until the advent of the supermarket, most towns and neighborhoods had at least one butcher shop, bakery, fishmonger, cheese store, and greengrocer. In many areas large grocery chains now coexist with small shops that are well worth visiting. You can ask for taste samples in the cheese store, get recipe advice from the butcher, and often have a cup of coffee with your fresh pastry in a bakery.

The convenience of one-stop shopping has helped grocery chains flourish in Denmark. Stores such as Irma, Kvickly, and Brugsen are cooperatives, dating back to the highly successful cooperative movement that started in Denmark in the late 19th century. Danish grocery stores are much like those in America, although you should expect to pay a coin deposit to use a grocery cart and plan to bag your own groceries. Customers often bring their own bags, and are usually charged for those provided by the store.

In addition to Danish products, most stores have a selection of international products, and also sell wine and beer. Organic products are very popular and are labeled *økologisk*.

About Street Eats

Hot dogs and international options such as falafel and shawarma (a popular Middle Eastern meat sandwich) are available on street corners in most larger cities. During the warmer months ice cream kiosks offer soft-serve, pre-made frozen treats, and scooped ice cream cones. Street vendors in Denmark are regulated by the same sanitation standards as restaurants, and must display the "smiley" mark showing their food safety rating (www.findsmiley.dk). Although it is highly unlikely that an outdoor food stall would sell anything not properly stored or cooked, you should use you own discretion in deciding whether to purchase snacks from a street vendor.

Weights, Measures, and International Regulations

Denmark uses the metric system. Products in a market are usually sold by the kilo or gram. However you may see some fruits and vegetables priced by the piece (*per stykke*).

The Danish currency is *kroner* (crowns), and amounts less than one *krone* are in *øre*. One *krone* equals 100 *øre*. You may find that some large stores, especially in Copenhagen, will accept euros. Credit and debit cards are widely used, and usually require a PIN number. Check with your credit card company before your trip to avoid this being a problem.

If you are considering bringing food back to the United States, check the Web site of the US Customs and Border Protection (www.cbp.gov) for current regulations, which are subject to change.

Resources

Suppliers of Danish Food Items

It is not easy to find suppliers of Danish foods in the United States and Canada, although in some cases you can substitute ingredients from other Scandinavian countries, or even Germany. We have chosen recipes for the *Tastes of Denmark* (p. 43) that use items easily available here. But if you would like to try to make some other Danish dishes—or an array of traditional *smørrebrød*—the suppliers listed below may be able to help you procure what you need, including the special pans needed to make *æbleskiver* and *rugbrød*. We have also included Danish bakeries that ship their goods, because we know that many Danes today no longer make their own *rugbrød* or *kringle* at home. The following food and specialty shops have online or mail-order businesses and some have brick-and-mortar retail shops as well.

Bendtsen's Bakery
3200 Washington Ave
Racine, WI 53405
262-633-0365
www.bendtsensbakery.com
(*kringle*)

Copenhagen Pastry
11113 Washington Blvd
Culver City, CA 90232
310-839-8900
www.copenhagenpastry.com
www.ryebreads.com
(*rugbrød*)

Danish Imports Online
167 South Parkview, Ste 7
Daly City, CA 94014
www.shop.danish-imports.com
(licorice, gummies, other candy)

Ingebretsens
1601 East Lake St
Minneapolis, MN 55497
800-279-9333
www.ingebretsens.com
(*æbleskiver* pans, kitchen supplies, cookbooks, non-perishables)

Larsen's Danish Bakery
8000 24th Ave NW
Seattle, WA 98117
800-626-8631
www.larsensbakery.com
(*kringle, kransekage*, other
   baked goods)

Nordic House
2709 San Pablo Ave
Berkeley, CA 94702
800-854-6435
www.nordichouse.com
(candy, kitchen supplies, cheese,
   æbleskiver pans, *flaeksesteg*)

Nordisk Import
903 Willeo Place
Marietta, GA 30068
770-594-7524
www.nordiskimport.com
(chocolate, candy, licorice,
   kammerjunkere, cheese,
   fish products)

O & H Danish Bakery
1841 Douglas Ave
Racine, WI 53402
800-709-4009
www.ohdanishbakery.com
(*kringle,* cakes, *rugbrød,* other
   baked goods)

Olsen's Village Bakery
1529 Mission Dr
Solvang, CA 93463
olsensdanishvillagebakery.com
(*kringle, kransekage, thebirkes*)

Orange Tree Imports
1721 Monroe St
Madison, WI 53711
888-245-1860
www.orangetreeimports.com
(*æbleskiver* pans, pullman loaf
   pans, **EAT SMART** guides)

Scandinavian Boutique
349 Main Ave
Norwalk, CT 06851
203-529-3244
www.scandinavianbutik.com
(*rugbrød*, herring, meat, cheese
   fish, home goods, candy)

Scandinavian Specialties
6719 15th Ave NW
Seattle, WA 98117
877-784-7020
www.scanspecialties.com
(meat, fish, cheese, *æbleskiver*
   pans, home goods)

Willy's Products
   Scandinavian Food Store
601 NW 38th Ave
Lauderhill, FL 33311
954-316-1350
www.scandinavianfoodstore.com
(meat, fish, *gravlaks*)

If you love Danish food and are interested in finding it in the US or Canada without having to cook it yourself, perhaps you'll find that there is a Danish ice cream shop, bakery, or restaurant somewhere near you. The following establishments are, for the most part, run by expat Danes or by second- or third-generation Danish-Americans. Some are extensions of establishments in Denmark. They have brought Danish delicacies like *smørrebrød* and *aebleskiver* to North America, which have found a welcome audience even if the customers have a hard time pronouncing the dishes! With the New Nordic movement gaining popularity nationally look for more chefs such as Noma co-founder Claus Meyer bringing this concept to North America.

West

Solvang, a city located two hours north of Los Angeles, is Danish for "sunny field" and was founded by a group of Danes in 1911 and incorporated as a city in 1985. Solvang is home to many Danish bakeries, restaurants, and museums including one devoted to Hans Christian Andersen. There is an annual Danish Days weekend in September and a *Julefest* in December.

Ingeborg's World Famous
   Danish Chocolates
1679 Copenhagen Dr
Solvang, CA 93463
805-688-5612
www.ingeborgs.com

Danish Mill Bakery, Inc
1682 Copenhagen Dr
Solvang, CA 93463
800-688-5805
www.danishmillbakery.com

Andersen's Danish Restaurant
   & Bakery
1106 State St
Santa Barbara, CA 93101
805-962-5085
www.andersenssantabarbara.com

The Solvang Baker
438 Alisal Rd
Solvang, CA 93463
805-688-4939
www.solvangbakery.com

Paradis (Danish ice cream)
5305 E 2nd St
Los Angeles, CA 90803
818-726-1847
www.paradis-icecream.com

Taste of Denmark
3401 Telegraph Ave
Oakland, CA 94609
510-420-8889
www.tastedenmark.com

Carlsbad Danish Bakery
2805 Roosevelt St
Carlsbad, CA 92008
760-729-6186
www.carlsbaddanish.com

Hygge Bakery
1106 S Hope St
Los Angeles, CA 90015
213-995-5022
www.hyggebakery.com

Taste of Denmark European Style Bakery
1901 S Kipling St
Lakewood, CO 80227
303-987-828
www.tasteofdenmark.net

Poul's Danish-American Bakery
770 N Tustin St
Orange, CA 92867
714-532-5101
www.pouls-bakery.com

Midwest

Elk Horn and nearby Kimballton, Iowa, are the largest Danish settlements in the rural US. Elk Horn is home to the Museum of Danish America and the Danish Villages, which features an operational windmill from Nørre Snede and a replica of the Little Mermaid sculpture.

Danish Inn Restaurant
4116 Main St
Elk Horn, IA 51531
712-764-4250
www.danishinnrestaurant.com

Kirsten's Danish Bakery
94 Burr Ridge Pkwy
Burr Ridge, IL 60527
630-655-2066
www.kirstensdanishbakery.com

East

Simply Scandinavian Foods
469 Stevens Ave
Portland, ME 04103
877-874-6759
www.simplyscandinavianfoods.com

The Danish Pastry House
205 Arlington St, Unit 4
Watertown, MA 02472
617-926-2747
www.danishpastryhouse.com

The Copenhagen
13 Laight St
New York, NY 10013
212-925-1313
www.thecopenhagennyc.com

Tørst Bar and Luksus Restaurant
615 Manhattan Ave
Brooklyn, NY 11222
718-389-6034
www.torstnyc.com

Out of Denmark
2275 S Federal Hwy
Delray Beach, FL 33483
561-276-2242
www.restaurantoutofdenmark.com

Canada

The Danish Canadian National Museum
   Coffee House (open seasonally)
35544 Range Rd 31
Spruce View, Alberta T0M 1V0
403-728-0019
www.danishcanadians.com

Hansens Danish Bakery Shop
1017 Pape Ave
Toronto, Ontario M4K 3V8
416-425-8877
www.danishpastry.ca

Mermaid Inn Restaurant
The Danish Canadian Club of Calgary
727-11th Ave SW
Calgary, Alberta
403-261-9774
www.danishclubcalgary.com

Karelia Kitchen
194 Bloor St West
Toronto, Ontario M6H 1N2
647-748-1194
www.kareliakitchen.com

Online, News, and Social Information

Although Danes are not one of the larger ethnic groups in North America, there are still resources here to keep up on Danish news, culture, and food. The following are a few select resources.

Eat Smart in Denmark Online

For up-to-date information on Danish food and cooking, please visit the *Eat Smart in Denmark* **Facebook** page. Here you'll find information on Danish food in the news as well as events and recipes.
   www.facebook.com/EatSmartInDenmark

The *Eat Smart in Denmark* **Pinterest** page has links and photos of traditional Danish cookware, food, and recipes.

    www.pinterest.com/Shoporangetree/danish-food-travel-from-the-eat-smart-in-denmark-b/

The **EAT SMART** Guides Web site for *Eat Smart in Denmark* maintains current information about Danish restaurants, bakeries, clubs, and Danish-American societies across North America. These clubs and societies promote Danish culture with events that feature Danish literature, art, music, and cuisine.

    www.eatsmartguides.com/denmark-resources.html

Danish-American Newspapers

The Danish Pioneer (*Den Danske Pioneer*)   www.thepdanishpioneer.com
The oldest Danish community newspaper in North America, "The Danish Pioneer" has been published since 1872, with articles written in both English and Danish.

Bien (The Bee)   www.biennews.com
A Danish-language newspaper published bi-weekly from California. Originally published in Norwegian, it came under Danish management in 1890.

Tours, Travel Advice, and Useful Organizations

You will find helpful information for planning your trip to Denmark on the Visit Denmark Web site (www.visitdenmark.com), which is the official Web site of the tourist board of Denmark. There is information about restaurants and lodging, and links to the home pages of different parts of the country.

    Wonderful Copenhagen (www.visitcopenhagen.com) is the best place to go for information about what to do in the capital city. No trip to Denmark would be complete without a few days in Copenhagen!

    Denmark.dk (www.denmark.dk) is the official Web site of Denmark. Here you can find plenty of information from blogs written by Americans to recommendations for new restaurants—and everything in between.

Denmark in the USA (http://usa.um.dk) is a Web site maintained by the Ministry of Foreign Affairs, and has information both about travel to Denmark as well as about Danish culture and events in the US.

If you'd like to visit Denmark but aren't sure where to start or would prefer not to plan a visit yourself, there are plenty of companies that offer guided tours of various lengths and destinations. These include Nordic Visitor (http://denmark.nordicvisitor.com), ScanAm (www.scandinaviantravel.com), and Scantours (www.scantours.net/products/region/denmark/38/).

Once you arrive in Copenhagen you can take a food tour of the city from Copenhagen Food Tours http://copenhagen.foodtours.eu/. They offer a 2-hour or 4-hour walking tour of the city where you'll taste the local cuisine along the way.

Don't want to walk and eat? Consider taking a cooking class in Copenhagen, where you can learn to bake the famous rye bread or whip up some tasty New Nordic dishes (http://cphgoodfood.dk/course_category/courses/).

Danish Government and Tourism Offices

Embassy of Denmark, USA
3200 Whitehaven St NW
Washington, DC 20008

Consulate General of Denmark
One Dag Hammarskjold Plaza
885 Second Ave, 18th Fl
New York, NY 10017-2201
212-223-4545

Consulate General of Denmark
875 N Michigan Ave, Ste 3950
Chicago, IL 60611
312-787-8780

Danish Tourist Board
PO Box 4649
Grand Central Station
New York, NY 10163-4649
212-885-9700

International Organizations

Two non-profit, international travel organizations, The Friendship Force and Servas, promote goodwill and understanding among people of different cultures. These organizations share similar ideals but operate somewhat differently. Friendship Force members travel in groups to host countries. Both itinerary and travel arrangements are made by a member acting as exchange director. These trips combine stays with a host family and group travel within the host country. Servas members travel independently and make their own contacts with fellow members in other countries, choosing hosts with attributes of interest from membership rosters.

For more information about membership in these groups:

Friendship Force International
127 Peachtree St, Ste 501
Atlanta, GA 30303
404-522-9490
www.thefriendshipforce.org

US Servas, Inc.
1125 16th St, Ste 201
Arcata, CA 95521
707-825-1714
info@usservas.org
www.usservas.org

Helpful Phrases

For Use in Restaurants and Food Markets

In the Restaurant

You will find the following Danish phrases useful in ordering food, learning more about the dish you ordered, and determining what specialties of a region are available. Each phrase also is written phonetically to help with pronunciation. Syllables in capital letters are accented. Note that the Danes do not have a word for "please," which is difficult for English-speakers to do without! You will find that Danes are pleased that you try to speak in Danish, even though almost all of them speak English.

DO YOU HAVE A MENU?	Har I en meny? *Hahr EE ehn meh-NEW?*
MAY I SEE THE MENU?	Kan jeg se menyen? *Kan yai say meh-NEW-ehn?*
WHAT DO YOU RECOMMEND TODAY?	Hvad anbefaler du? *Vah AHN-beh-fah-lehr dew?*
DO YOU HAVE . . . HERE? (ADD AN ITEM FROM THE *MENU GUIDE* OR THE *FOODS & FLAVORS GUIDE*.)	Har du . . . her? *Hahr dew . . . hehr?*

Helpful Phrases

WHAT IS THE "SPECIAL" FOR TODAY?	Hvad er dagens ret? *Vah air DAY-ehns reht?*
DO YOU HAVE ANY SPECIAL LOCAL DISHES?	Har I nogle lokale retter? *Hahr EE now-leh lo-KAHL-leh REHT-ehr?*
IS THIS DISH SPICY?	Er denne ret stærkt krydret? *Air DEHN-eh REHT stehrkt KRID-reht?*
I/WE WOULD LIKE TO ORDER . . .	Jeg / Vi vil gerne bestille . . . *Yai / Vee vill GEHRN-eh beh-STILL-eh . . .*
WHAT ARE THE INGREDIENTS IN THIS DISH?	Hvilke ingredienser er i denne ret? *VILL-keh in-GREH-dee-EHN-sehr air ee DEHN-eh REHT?*
WHAT ARE THE SEASONINGS IN THIS DISH?	Hvilke krydderier er i denne ret? *VILL-keh KRID-dehr-eer air ee DEHN-eh REHT?*
THANK YOU VERY MUCH. THE FOOD IS DELICIOUS.	Mange tak. Maden smager dejlig. *MAHNG-eh tahk. MAHL-en SMAY-er DIY-lee.*

In the Market

The following phrases will help you make purchases and learn more about unfamiliar produce, spices, and herbs.

WHAT ARE THE LOCAL FRUITS AND VEGETABLES?

Hvilke frugter og grønsager dyrkes i området?
VILL-keh FRUHK-tehr oh GROHN-say-ehr DEWRK-iss ee ohm-ROH-deh?

WHAT IS THIS CALLED?

Hvad hedder det?
Vah HEH-der deh?

DO YOU SELL . . . HERE?
(ADD AN ITEM FROM THE *FOODS & FLAVORS GUIDE.*)

Har du . . . her?
HAHR dew . . . hehr?

MAY I TASTE THIS?

Må jeg smage det?
Moh yai SMAY-eh deh?

WHERE CAN I BUY FRESH . . . ?

Hvor kan jeg købe frisk . . . ?
Vohr kahn yai KOO-beh frisk . . . ?

HOW MUCH IS THIS PER KILOGRAM?

Hvad koster det per kilo?
Vah KOH-stehr day pehr KEE-loh?

I WOULD LIKE TO BUY ¼ KILO OF THAT.

Jeg vil gerne have et kvart kilo af det.
Yai vill GEHRN-eh hah eht kvahrt KEE-loh ahv deh.

MAY I PHOTOGRAPH THAT?

Må jeg tage et billede af det?
Moh yai tah eht BILL-eh-theh ahv day?

Other Useful Phrases

Sometimes it helps to see in writing a word or phrase that is said to you in Danish, because certain letters sound distinctly different in English than in Danish. You may be familiar with the word and its Danish translation but less familiar with its pronunciation. The following phrase comes in handy if you want to see the word or phrase you are hearing.

PLEASE WRITE IT ON MY PIECE OF PAPER.

Vil du være så venlig at skrive det ned for mig, tak?

Vill dew VAIR so VEN-lee at SKREEV-eh deh NEHD for mai, tahk?

Interested in bringing home books about Danish food?

WHERE CAN I BUY A DANISH COOKBOOK IN ENGLISH?

Hvor kan jeg købe en dansk kogebog på engelsk?

Vohr kahn yai KEH-beh ehn dansk KOH-eh-boh poh EHNG-ehlsk?

And, of course, the following phrases also are useful to know.

WHERE IS THE RESTROOM?

Hvor er toilettet?

Vohr air toh-ah-LEH-teh?

MAY I HAVE THE CHECK, PLEASE?

Må jeg bede om regningen, tak.

Moh yai BAY-the om RYE-ning-ehn, tahk.

DO YOU ACCEPT CREDIT CARDS?

Tar du kreditkort?

Tahr dew KREH-deet-kohrt?

Menu Guide

Here is an alphabetical listing of Danish dishes, along with baked goods, drinks, sausages, and cheese. Use this *Menu Guide* as a resource when ordering from a menu in a restaurant, eating at a food cart, or shopping in a grocery store for prepared foods. You will find individual ingredients in the *Foods & Flavors Guide* that follows.

Please note that the Danish alphabet has 29 letters, so after the familiar a–z you will find words that begin with the vowels æ, ø, and å. We have used the Danish alphabetical order, so you will find *gåsesteg,* for example, after *gullash.* Note that in English the letter æ is sometimes written as ae, and å as aa.

Danish has two genders, the common and neuter. In singular form the suffixes *–en* (common gender) and *–et* (neuter gender) mean "the." Plurals are made by adding *–er* or *–e* at the end of a noun. Possessives are made by simply adding *–s*, as in *mormors* for "grandmother's." Adjectives describing a singular noun either have no suffix (common gender) or end in *–t* (neuter gender), and end in *–e* or *–ede* when describing a plural noun. This glossary lists the singular form of all words unless there is a significant exception to these grammatical rules.

Danes love to string words together to make a single word, such as the dessert *kærnemælkskoldskål*, which is, literally, "buttermilk-cold-bowl." If you are unsure of the meaning of a word not listed in this glossary, try taking it apart and seeing if you can find the individual parts in the *Foods & Flavors Guide*. It is also helpful to know the following prepositions and conjunctions:

det, den, de the	**i** in	**med** with
og and	**på** on	**uden** without

Danes generally eat their meals at about the same time as Americans—that is, breakfast before work or school, lunch at noon, and dinner around 6:00. A typical day starts with a *morgenmad* (breakfast) of milk or yogurt on cold cereal, muesli, or oatmeal (eaten either hot or uncooked), or a more traditional meal of bread with cheese or jam, accompanied by coffee or tea. Slices of cheeses ranging from mild to strong are eaten on the omnipresent Danish *rugbrød* (thin-sliced pumpernickel rye bread; see recipe, p. 45), *franskbrød* (white bread), or bakery rolls. *Rugbrød*, which is very high in fiber, has long been a staple of the Danish diet, and is eaten for both breakfast and lunch. Refined white bread used to be reserved for special occasions, although this is changing. Blocks of cheese are usually put on the table so that each can slice his own—which can lead to smelly fingers if the cheese is strong. Some hotels have solved this problem by providing a special rotating cutter that allows guests to slice cheese without touching the cheese. Hotels may also offer sliced ham or sausage, as well as boiled eggs.

On special occasions fresh rolls and pastry from the local bakery may magically appear on the breakfast table, usually the result of someone taking an early bike ride to the local *bageri* (bakery). If both savory and sweet options are offered, it is traditional to eat the cheese or meat before enjoying the pastry.

Brunch is a relatively new concept in Denmark that has been enthusiastically embraced, and some restaurants serve brunch into the afternoon on both weekdays and weekends. Danish brunch might include cheese, bread, pastries, *pandekager* (crepe-like pancakes), yogurt, fruit, bacon and sausage, and a variety of egg dishes.

The Danes love coffee, and a typical day may include a *kaffepause* (coffee break) in the morning and another one in the afternoon, called *eftermiddagskaffe*. Pastry or some other sweet is often served with coffee, especially in the afternoon. Coffee shops in Denmark have evolved into an important part of the social scene as a popular place for friends to meet.

Frokost (lunch) is often brought from home (in a *madpakke*) rather than purchased in a restaurant, although some schools and larger workplaces provide excellent cafeterias. There was a time when lunch in Denmark always meant *smørrebrød,* the classic Danish open-faced sandwiches. Today the options are much more varied, although sandwiches with a top and bottom piece of bread are still the exception rather than the rule.

A special lunch in the Danish tradition is *det kolde bord* (literally, "the cold table"), which is often referred to somewhat erroneously in English by the Swedish word *smörgåsbord*. The Danish version of a *smörgåsbord* is sometimes called *det store kolde bord*, meaning "the grand cold table," because of the large variety of dishes on the buffet. Although the name includes the word "cold," there are often warm dishes as well. It is traditional to start with marinated herring, then to have seafood dishes such as salmon, fried plaice, or shrimp, followed by cold meats, warm meats, egg or vegetable toppings, and then cheese. There are many traditional *smørrebrød* combinations involving specific *pålæg* (main toppings), *tilbehør* (garnishes) such as pickled beets, grated horseradish, chopped onions, potato salad, and crispy onions, and different types of bread. Those not familiar with *smørrebrød* would do well to ask for some guidance.

It is traditional to start a formal lunch with the host raising a small glass of aquavit (*snaps*), and welcoming guests with the toast, "*Skål!*" Guests should raise their glasses and make eye contact with one another before taking a sip of the potent drink and starting to eat. Beer is served throughout the meal, sometimes accompanied by more *snaps*.

For dinner (called *middag* or *aftensmad*), Danes traditionally have a main course of meat, fish, or chicken—with potatoes—usually accompanied by a vegetable, cucumber salad, and/or pickled red cabbage. Although this is changing, there are few traditional hot Danish meals that don't feature potatoes in some form—in fact we once counted them served five different ways at an dinner in an old-fashioned inn.

A formal Danish dinner will usually start with an appetizer course featuring *gravad laks* (marinated salmon; see recipe, p. 44), fish roe, *rejer* (small shrimp), or some other type of seafood. It is customary to use a smaller plate on top of the dinner plate for the appetizer course, and this plate is removed before the main course is served.

Dessert at the table will be a "pudding" in the British manner—ice cream, mousse, or porridge. Favorite Danish desserts include *æblekage* (apple charlotte; see recipe, p. 62), *kærnemælkskoldskål* (buttermilk dessert, see recipe, p. 63), *rødgrød med fløde* (red berry porridge with cream; see recipe, p. 65), *rabarbertrifli* (rhubarb trifle; see recipe, p. 66), and *citronfromage* (lemon mousse; see recipe, p. 68).

In typical Danish style, this dessert course is followed by more sweets served away from the table together with coffee. Danes do not drink coffee with their dinner, and it is worth noting that the coffee served after dinner is not usually decaffeinated. *Aftenskaffe* (evening coffee) is often enjoyed in the living room, together with chocolates and pastries. Guests are sometimes invited for just *aftenskaffe*, instead of dinner, to celebrate a special occasion such as a birthday.

Natmad ("night meal") is a midnight snack served late in the evening during a wedding or formal party, or after a concert or play. It is also sometimes called a *souper*, using the French term, and soup is sometimes a feature of the *natmad*. Other options include egg dishes, pizza, meatballs, or sausages. If you are invited to an evening event hosted by the queen, there may be a *souper* reception—but pizza is unlikely to be on the menu.

When dining in a restaurant it is useful to know that the *moms* (tax) and *betjening* or *drikkepenge* (service charge or tip) are included in the bill. If the service is particularly good, however, it is appreciated if you round up on your credit card payment or leave a few *kroner* of change for the waiter.

Snaps and beer are traditional with a big lunch, and wine is often served with dinner. Danes enjoy drinking socially, with many toasts at a festive meal, and liqueur often served with the coffee afterwards. The legal drinking age is 16, and most young Danes have their first experience with alcohol before that time. But keep in mind that there is a zero tolerance policy for drunk driving in Denmark. Non-alcoholic options include *sodavand* (soda) and *saftevand* (fruit juice concentrate diluted with water). Tap water is generally quite safe to drink throughout the country. However, some travelers have trouble adjusting to local differences in water. If that is the case, you would do well to use bottled water.

Getting together with Danes is often an opportunity to experience the very Danish concept of *hygge*, which is loosely translated as "coziness." The extensive use of candles during the long, dark, winter months helps create a *hyggelig* (cozy) atmosphere. Relaxing with friends over a drink, or a cup of coffee, can also be *hyggelig*. Danes put a great deal of effort into making their homes comfortable and inviting, and were into "nesting" before that was hip in the US. This is one reason that they don't eat out as much as we do—the other being the high cost of restaurant meals, which include the addition of *moms* (value added tax) of about 25%.

If you are lucky enough to be invited to be a guest in a Danish home, arrive promptly and bring a gift such as flowers, chocolate, wine, or perhaps something from your home state. Many households prefer to have guests remove their shoes, so you might check in advance to make sure your socks are in good order (or bring a pair of house slippers). Plan on staying for an extended time, as meals are eaten slowly, and there is often after-dinner coffee in the living room.

Danes don't usually snack on hors d'oeuvres before going to the table. When the meal is ready you will be shown to your place at the table, generally with a woman to the right of a man. (In formal dining the person next to you is not your spouse, so you have to make conversation with someone you may not know well.) The host or hostess will usually say *værsgo* (help yourself) when the first course is on the table, but often a toast precedes the first bite. Danes use the continental dining style with the knife in the right hand and the fork in the left. It is polite to try a bit of everything, and to show that you are finished by placing your knife and fork together on the side of the plate.

Before getting up from the table at the end of the meal, thank your host and whoever prepared the meal by saying, *"Tak for mad"* [tahk for MALD], which means, "Thank you for this meal." And don't forget to send a thank-you note, or at least to say, *"Tak for sidst"* [tahk for SEEST]—"Thanks for the last time"— the next time you see your host. These courtesies will go a long way toward impressing everyone with your inside knowledge of Danish culture.

A few notes about healthy eating while in Denmark: Vegetarianism is becoming more common among young Danes. However it can be a challenge to get enough protein, since most traditional lunch and dinner dishes include meat, poultry, or fish. Even a soup made with peas may contain some pork. Ethnic eateries offer better options, and larger cities have excellent vegetarian restaurants. When planning to eat out, or in a Danish home, check in advance to see if there will be foods that you can enjoy.

Food hygiene has always been a source of pride in Denmark, and this has been taken to a new level with the "smiley scheme." Every retail food enterprise must exhibit one of four smiley faces in a prominent place visible to consumers, together with the inspection report that is summarized by the smiling (or frowning) symbol. Enterprises with hazardous  conditions are closed until the problem can be fixed, but those who have a flawless inspection history earn the right to display the Elite Smiley. You can find information about the Ministry of Food, Agriculture and Fisheries' program at www.findsmiley.dk.

Considering that Denmark recently imposed a "fat tax" (repealed one year later) on foods such as cheese and butter, and that the Danish population in general appears trim and fit, you might think that all Danish food is healthy. Not so! In fact, much of their food is fairly high in fat. However, Danes are very active, don't snack between meals, and also tend to eat smaller portions than Americans. You'll see some items marked with "healthy choice" in this *Menu Guide*. In general healthy options are fish dishes that are not fried, *rugbrød* (rye bread), and anything taking advantage of the abundance of fruits and vegetables. However, don't be surprised to have a cream sauce served on the fish or a butter sauce on the vegetables. We think it's best to enjoy the food while you're there but also to enjoy the active culture of Denmark by renting a bike or going for a long walk. Do as the natives do, and you'll be fine!

abemad fruit salad made with whipped cream. The famous Danish sense of humor is at work in the name of this dish, which literally means "monkey food."

NATIONAL FAVORITE **agurkesalat** sweet-and-sour marinated cucumber salad. Used as a side dish or as a garnish on *smørrebrød*, *agurkesalat* also refers to lightly pickled sliced cucumbers served on hot dogs. See recipe, page 57.

REGIONAL SPECIALTY **Amagergryde** stew made of ham or smoked pork with potatoes, peas, and carrots. Named for Amager, the island on which Copenhagen is partially situated. In Jutland this dish is called *ruskomsnusk*, which means "hodgepodge."

andebryst duck breast, often served with red cabbage.

aristokrater crisp little cookies baked from thin slices of chilled dough. The name literally means "aristocrats."

DELICIOUS **arme ridder** French toast served with jam as a dessert, not for breakfast. The literal meaning of the name is "poor knights."

HEALTHY CHOICE **bagt torsk** baked cod. See recipe, page 55.

REGIONAL SPECIALTY **bakskuld** salted, dried common dab fish (*Limanda limanda*), which is fried and served on *rugbrød* with *remoulade*. *Bakskuld* is a specialty of Fanø, an island off the coast of southwestern Denmark.

bedstefars skæg cake topped with jam (usually raspberry) and meringue. The cake's name means "Grandfather's beard."

TRADITIONAL DISH **benløse fugle** boneless veal cutlets flattened and rolled up around lard, carrots, and parsley. After browning the meat is simmered in beef stock. It is served with a gravy made of this stock with cream and *ribsgelé* (red currant jelly) added. The name literally means "boneless birds."

REGIONAL SPECIALTY **bidesild** herring taken raw from the salting barrel, a traditional Zealand delicacy. The name means "bite herring" because of the way it is eaten.

bidesild og fedtemad bite herring served with raw onion and *rugbrød* covered with pork fat.

VERY POPULAR **biksemad** hash made up of leftover meat, potatoes, onions, and gravy, served with a fried egg on top. The name literally means "food thrown together." Usually served with pickled beets and Worcestershire sauce, HP sauce, or ketchup, often with *rugbrød* on the side.

birkes pastry. See *thebirkes*.

blodpølse sausage made up of pig's blood and fat from the butcher, combined with rye, hulled barley seeds, brown sugar, salt, and spices such as cardamom and cinnamon. Boiled, sliced, and served warm with apples, cinnamon, syrup, and either melted butter or fat.

blomme i madeira plums cooked in sugar and Madeira wine; also a chocolate-covered plum and marzipan candy by Anton Berg.

blommekage plum cake with cardamom.

blød nougat soft brown nougat that can be eaten or used in baking. See *nougat*.

bløde løg onions sautéed until soft. Traditionally eaten on top of a ground meat burger that is served with potatoes, gravy, and pickled beets.

blødkogt æg soft-boiled egg.

boller rolls or meatballs.

boller i karry pork meatballs in a curry sauce with onions, served with rice.

bondepige med slør "veiled farm girl." See *æblekage*.

brun sovs brown gravy or sauce, made by adding a mixture of flour and water or milk to thicken the beef stock. Brown coloring is often added to darken the gravy. Served with boiled potatoes. Also called *brun sauce*.

brune kager spiced round or rectangular "brown cookies" made with brown sugar, syrup, and spices such as cinnamon and cloves. This cookie, which dates back to the Middle Ages, is traditionally decorated with slices of almond. It was earlier known as a *peberkage* (pepper cake) because it originally contained pepper. Also spelled *brunkager*.

brunede kartofler caramelized potatoes made by coating boiled potatoes in melted white sugar and butter that has been allowed to caramelize. Served for Christmas with duck, goose, or pork roast. Also called *sukkerbrunede kartofler*.

brunkål browned green cabbage.

brunsviger a sheet cake, made from sponge cake and topped with a mixture of melted brown sugar and butter. The traditional birthday cake on Fyn and in Northern Jutland.

brændende kærlighed mashed potatoes made with butter, whole milk or cream, and salt, then topped with chives. An indentation is made in the mashed potatoes to form a well for bacon cubes that have been fried with sliced onions. Served with pickled beets. The English translation of the name for this traditional peasant dish is "burning love."

brændte mandler sugar-coated roasted almonds.

byggrød barley porridge.

bøf tartar beef tartar, made from raw ground or scraped beef and served with a raw egg yolk, capers, grated horseradish, and chopped raw onions. Also called simply *tartar*.

DELICIOUS **chokolade bolle** chocolate glazed pastry.

DELICIOUS **citronfromage** lemon mousse, formerly a traditional Sunday dinner dessert. See recipe, page 68.

citronmarineret laks lemon-marinated salmon.

citronmåne round, single-layer cake with a lemon glaze, sometimes made as a half a circle (*citronhalvmåne*). "Lemon moon" is said to be a favorite of the Danish police force.

cocktailpølser little cocktail sausages. Sometimes served *i svøb* (wrapped in bacon).

DELICIOUS **cremebolle** large, round, filled cream puff with icing on top. Also known as *vandbakkelse* and *fastelavnsbolle,* these were once only eaten at *Fastelavn* time, but are now available year-round.

NATIONAL FAVORITE **Dagmartærte** buttery pastry (*smørkage*) that can be either round or rectangular. Named for Queen Dagmar (1186–1212), the *Dagmartærte* is not really a tart; it belongs to the group of pastries called *wienerbrød*.

NATIONAL FAVORITE **dansk bøf** Danish-style hamburger (*hakkebøf*), made of ground beef and served hot with potatoes and pickled beets. Always served with sautéed onions (*bløde løg*). Also called *hakkebøf*.

dildsovs dill sauce made with stock, vinegar or lemon juice, butter, egg yolk, and thickening.

drømmekage fra Brovst coconut-topped coffee cake from the Jutland town of Brovst. The name of this popular cake, which was created as part of an event for housewives in 1960, literally means "dream cake."

dyrefilet med kirsebær sovs venison tenderloins served with cherry sauce.

EXCELLENT **dyrlægens natmad** *smørrebrød* made of rye bread with a layer of liver pâté, a slice of salted beef, and a slice of meat jelly. Decorated with onions and garden cress. Named "The Veterinarian's Midnight Snack" in the 1920s by Ida Davidsen's Restaurant in honor of a regular customer's daily order. See recipe, page 47.

engelsk bøf flank steak, served with sautéed onions (*bløde løg*) and boiled potatoes.

Fanø smørrebrød *smørrebrød* made on white bread and cut into wedge shapes. Fanø is an island off the west coast of Jutland.. **REGIONAL SPECIALTY**

fars ground veal and/or pork mixed with eggs, flour, broth, or milk, usually the basis for *frikadeller* or a stuffing. See also *fiskefars*.

Fastelavnsbolle special glazed yeast bun for the Shrovetide season. After the dough has been allowed to rise, it is divided into individual portions. *Fastelavnsboller* can be filled with pieces of dried fruit or cake crème before baking or filled afterwards with whipped cream. The tradition of putting dried fruit in these buns is specific to the Jutland peninsula. **HOLIDAY FAVORITE**

fedtebrød iced cookies made with coconut. (Also refers to *rugbrød* coated with a layer of pork fat.) **TASTY**

finker minced boiled pork heart, liver, and kidney. The name literally means "finches."

finsk brød rectangular holiday shortbread cookie dusted with coarse sugar. The name means "Finnish bread."

fiskeboller fish dumplings, often served in tomato soup, which can be made from any minced white fish. **HEALTHY CHOICE**

fiskefars minced fish mixed with milk or cream, eggs, and flour.

fiskefrikadeller fish balls or cakes, made by mixing minced fish with flour or bread crumbs, egg yolk, spices, milk, and water. The mixture is then formed into cakes and either baked, grilled, or fried. **VERY POPULAR**

fiskesuppe fish soup. See page 52 for a recipe for Viking fish soup.

flæskesteg med svær pork roast with the skin on, oven-roasted in a water bath, and served with the crackling, along with pickled red cabbage, gravy, and either boiled or caramelized potatoes. Often served on Christmas Eve or for Christmas lunch. **NATIONAL FAVORITE**

flødebolle chocolate-covered confection often added on the top of an ice cream cone. Although the name means "cream ball," a *flødebolle* is actually a slice of wafer (or marzipan) topped with a filling made of whipped egg whites and sugar, then coated with dark chocolate. **DELICIOUS**

flødekager various pastries made with whipped cream filling (for example, *kartoffelkage*, *gåsebryst*, *napoleonskage*, *Tivoli kage*).

flødekartofler scalloped potatoes.

fløderand ring-shaped, molded cream dessert served with a tart jam sauce. May also contain caramel.

NATIONAL FAVORITE   **forloren hare med ribs** meatloaf made from ground beef and pork and wrapped in strips of bacon. Served with gravy that includes *ribsgelé* (red currant jelly). Literally, "mock hare," this dish takes its name from the fact that the red currant jelly sauce is a common way of serving hare—although mock hare is by far the more popular dish.

ELEGANT   **forloren skildpadde** mock turtle stew made from a calf's head and flavored with sherry. It is served with veal or pork meatballs (*kødboller*) and fish balls (*fiskeboller*), garnished with hard-boiled egg halves (*smilende æg*).

NATIONAL FAVORITE   **forårsruller** Chinese spring rolls.

fragilite square cake made of two thin layers of macaroon filled with a mocha cream. Despite its French name, this cake originated in Denmark in 1910.

fransk hotdog French hot dog, a hot dog that is inserted into a hollowed-out baguette seasoned with a tangy mayonnaise sauce.

POPULAR   **franske vafler** pastry that is two oval *mille feuille* cookies with buttercream in the center. The name literally means "French waffles," although these are not really waffles.

NATIONAL FAVORITE   **frikadeller** meatballs of ground veal and pork seasoned with onion, salt, and pepper and browned in butter. Served hot with boiled potatoes and brown gravy, or sliced cold on an open-faced sandwich. The term *frikadeller* is used to describe meatballs, usually of pork, in Germany and other European countries, but these variations are not the same as Danish *frikadeller*. See recipe, page 48.

NATIONAL FAVORITE   **frugtsalat** fresh, chopped fruit salad, served with a *råcreme* (see *Foods & Flavor Guide*) as a summer dessert (also called *abemad*).

frugtsuppe warm fruit soup.

DELICIOUS   **frøsnapper** a twisted pastry with sesame and poppy seeds on top. The Copenhagen version is sweet, containing *remonce,* whereas in Jutland it is more like a bread.

TASTY   **Gamle Ole** very strong aged cheese. The name means "Old Ole."

gammeldags is old-fashioned (hand-packed) ice cream in a homemade cone.

NATIONAL FAVORITE   **gammeldags kylling** braised chicken stuffed with parsley, rubbed with salt and pepper and cooked on the stovetop or in the oven. Served with new potatoes and pickled cucumber salad. Also called *stegt kylling.* See recipe, page 56.

gammeldags oksesteg beef pot roast. See *oksesteg.*

gammeldags æblekage apple pudding. See *æblekage*.

gemyse accompanying vegetable(s).

gløgg hot mulled wine made with red wine, Port, liqueur, oranges, brown sugar, and spices. See recipe, page 43. NATIONAL FAVORITE

gode råd decorative Southern Jutland cookie made using a special press similar to the Norwegian *krumkake* iron. The name means "good advice." REGIONAL SPECIALTY

gravad laks raw salmon salted and marinated in dill, served with a dill-mustard sauce called *rævsovs*. See recipe, page 44. HEALTHY CHOICE

grillkylling rotisserie chicken.

grovbirkes a flaky, whole-grain breakfast puff pastry topped with poppy seeds. See also *thebirkes*.

Grundlovsdessert old-fashioned traditional Constitution Day (June 5) dessert made with fresh rhubarb and whipping cream.

grønlangkål creamed, chopped curly kale, often served with ham and *brunede kartofler* (caramelized potatoes) on January 5th to celebrate Twelfth Night. See recipe, page 60. HOLIDAY FAVORITE

gule ærter split pea soup made from dried yellow peas and a ham bone or pork shoulder. Can be served with sausage, boiled pork belly (*kogt flæsk*), pickled beets, *rugbrød,* and mustard. Traditional in the fall and winter. See recipe, page 51. NATIONAL FAVORITE

gullash goulash.

gås med svesker og æbler roast goose stuffed with prunes and apples, traditionally served on Christmas Eve.

gåsebryst pastry made by topping a piece of puff pastry with prune marmalade, a dab of vanilla cream, and a thick layer of whipped cream, and then covering it with marzipan. The pastry gets its name from its "goose breast" shape. POPULAR

gåsesteg roast goose.

H. C. Andersens smørrebrød an open-faced sandwich said to be a favorite of Hans Christian Andersen. Bread topped with crisp bacon, tomato, and liver pâté, garnished with meat jelly.

hakkebøf med bløde løg minced or ground beef, usually served with soft, slightly caramelized onions (*bløde løg*), boiled potatoes, and brown sauce. Also called *dansk bøf*. GOOD CHOICE

hamburgerryg smoked saddle of pork, boiled before serving. NATIONAL FAVORITE

hasselback kartofler potatoes that are baked after being peeled and then scored partway through.

havregrød hot oatmeal porridge. HEALTHY CHOICE

HEALTHY CHOICE **helleflynderkoteletter med persillesovs** halibut fillets served with parsley sauce.

NATIONAL FAVORITE **hindbærsnitter** thin, crisp, two-layer pastry bars filled with raspberry preserves and topped with icing and sprinkles.

DELICIOUS **hjemrøget laks** salmon smoked in the kitchen. See also *røget laks*.

hjerter i flødesovs boiled or fried pig hearts in cream sauce, served with potatoes.

hold-kæft bolcher large hard candies. Literally called, "shut up drops." Also called (more politely) *hold-mund bolsjer*.

honninghjerter heart-shaped cookies flavored with honey and coated with chocolate. The southern Jutland town of Christiansfeld is well known for its *honninghjerter*, which are related to the German *lebkuchen*. Also called *honningkage*.

horn crescent-shaped roll.

POPULAR **hotdog** hot dog.

hovedret main course.

hvedeknopper cardamon wheat rolls eaten warm on the evening before *Store Bededag*, or Great Prayer Day. This holiday combines several lesser holy days into one larger one on the fourth Friday after Easter. Since bakers couldn't work on the holiday itself, the rolls were baked on Thursday to be warmed up or toasted on Friday, but now they are eaten Thursday evening. *Hvedeknopper* are also called *varme hveder*.

hvælling gruel, porridge.

højkål curly kale, boiled and chopped, then browned in fat from pork roast and served with cubes of potato.

HEALTHY CHOICE **hønsekødssuppe** chicken soup, served with dumplings (*melboller*), small meatballs, and chopped vegetables.

TASTY **hønsesalat** chicken salad, often used as *pålæg*.

håndmad *smørrebrød* picked up to be eaten, as opposed to those that require a knife and fork. Literally, "hand meal."

i svøb in swaddling, referring to a hot dog wrapped in bacon.

ingenting small cookie with meringue on top from Southern Jutland. The name means "nothing."

POPULAR **italiensk salat** peas, asparagus, and carrots in a mayonnaise dressing, often paired with slices of baked ham on an open-faced sandwich. The name "Italian salad" is thought to come from the colors of the Italian flag, although the dish is actually of Danish origin and dates back to the 1930s.

jordbær med fløde strawberries in heavy cream, a summer favorite.

jordbærtærte strawberry tart with a shortbread crust, a layer of **GOOD CHOICE**
dark chocolate, a layer of cake creme, strawberries, and a glaze.
A seasonal specialty.

julekage Christmas fruit cake.

jægergryde hunter's stew, a dish made with pork tenderloin or beef.

jødekager thin, round Christmas cookies with cardamom flavoring **HOLIDAY FAVORITE**
and topped with cinnamon sugar and almonds. The name
literally means "Jewish cakes," and these cookies were probably
named after a similar treat from the Jewish bakeries in Copenhagen.

kaffebrød med makron pastry made from toasted bread (similar
to a Zwieback) with an almond glaze on top.

kaffepunch coffee spiked with *snaps*. Associated with the sailors' **REGIONAL SPECIALTY**
taverns on the coast of Jutland.

kagekone woman-shaped cake, for a child's birthday.

kagemand man-shaped cake, for a child's birthday.

Kaj kage cream-topped pastry made by topping a cookie with
green marzipan shaped like a frog's head. Named after a
character in a popular Danish children's TV program. Also
spelled as one word: *Kajkage*.

kalvebryst breast of veal, served with a dill or horseradish sauce.

kalvefrikassè veal or lamb casserole with boiled carrots, leeks, **TRADITIONAL DISH**
and peas (sometimes with asparagus) in white sauce with
parsley. Served with small, white boiled potatoes.

kalveleverpostej calf's liver pâté.

kammerjunker small sweet rusk-like cookies. "Valet's cookies"
were traditionally used as Christmas tree ornaments, and now
are served on top of cold buttermilk soup (a dessert). They are
similar to American Nilla Wafers, but not as sweet.

kanelsnurrer cinnamon swirl buns, cinnamon rolls. The pastry is **EXCELLENT**
also called *kanelsnegle*, which literally means "cinnamon snail."
See also *snegl*.

karbonader rissoles; patties of ground veal and pork seasoned,
breaded, and fried. Served with freshly grated horseradish,
capers, gravy, creamed peas and carrots, and boiled potatoes.
Also called *krebinetter*.

karrysild marinated herring in a curry mayonnaise sauce. See **DELICIOUS**
recipe, page 47.

karrytorsk cod in cream sauce seasoned with curry, a specialty **REGIONAL SPECIALTY**
from Gilleleje in northern Zealand.

GOOD CHOICE **kartoffelkage** an oval éclair filled with cream, topped with a layer of marzipan and dusted with cocoa powder to make it look like a potato. It is therefore called a "potato cake," even though there is no potato among the ingredients.

kartoffelmad *smørrebrød* featuring slices of cold boiled potatoes, often garnished with mayonnaise and crispy onions.

kartoffelmos mashed potatoes.

TASTY **kartoffelsalat** potato salad served *varm* (warm; made with vinegar) or *kold* (cold; made with mayonnaise).

POPULAR **kartoffelsuppe med bacon og purløg** creamy potato soup served with crisp bacon bits and chopped chives.

kiksekage a cake made by layering vanilla cookies in a baking dish with a mixture of melted chocolate with condensed milk, butter, and vanilla. It is chilled, not baked.

kirsebær sovs hot cherry sauce, served on rice pudding on Christmas Eve. See recipe, page 64.

hjemrøget laks salmon smoked at home on the stovetop.

klatkage fried leftover rice pudding, porridge, or potatoes. A well is made in the center for a pat of butter, and then it is sprinkled with cinnamon. Often served with jam.

HOLIDAY FAVORITE **klejner** traditional Christmas cookies twisted into a bow before frying. These fried cookies date back to the 1300s, long before Danish homes had ovens for baking.

klipfisk salted, dried cod.

HEALTHY CHOICE **knækbrød** crispbread.

kogt flæsk boiled pork belly.

kogt torsk i sennepssauce poached cod with mustard sauce. Usually served with pickled beets and chopped hardboiled eggs.

kogt æg boiled egg.

NATIONAL FAVORITE **koldskål** cold buttermilk soup—a dessert soup made by whipping raw eggs into chilled fresh buttermilk, lightly seasoned with sugar and lemon. Similar to eggnog but served as a dessert, mostly in the summer. Served topped with *kammerjunker*. Also called *kærnemælkskoldskål*. See recipe, page 63.

koldt bord buffet (sometimes called a *smorgasbord*, which is a Swedish term) of many different dishes (meats, fish—especially different varieties of herring—cheese, pâtés, salads) used to make up one's own *smørrebrød*. Despite the name, which means the cold table, some of the dishes may be served warm. *Det store kolde bord* means "a big buffet."

DELICIOUS **konditorkager** cakes made by a fancy bakery called a *konditori*.

POPULAR **Kongen af Danmark** King of Denmark anise-flavored hard candies.

koteletter med champignon pork chops with creamed mushrooms. Sometimes seen as *svinekoteletter med champignon*.

kransekage almond pastry cake glazed with a drizzle of icing. Can be made into cookies (sometimes with chocolate on the bottom) or shaped into a tower of concentric rings or a cornucopia. *Kransekage* has a long tradition as a Danish wedding cake, but is now also served on New Year's Eve and for special birthdays and other events. **NATIONAL FAVORITE**

krebinetter meat rissoles. See *karbonader*.

kringle pretzel-shaped pastry that is the symbol of Danish bakeries. See also *wienerbrød*. **NATIONAL FAVORITE**

kronhjort red deer (*Cervus elaphus*), venison.

kryddersild spiced marinated herring.

kræmmerhus cone-shaped cookie served filled with whipped cream and either fruit or jam. *Kræmmerhus* also refers to paper cones that are filled with treats and hung on the Christmas tree.

kys meringue "kiss."

kærnemælkskoldskål cold buttermilk dessert soup. See *koldskål*. See recipe, page 63. **NATIONAL FAVORITE**

kødboller boiled meatballs made of pork or veal. See also *frikadeller*, which are fried meatballs.

kåldolmere stuffed cabbage rolls filled with a minced pork mixture.

kålpølser Southern Jutland pork sausage served with creamed kale (hence the name "cabbage sausage"). **REGIONAL SPECIALTY**

labskovs stew or hash. See *skipperlabskovs*.

lagkage layered cake, often not frosted on the sides. *Fødselsdagslagkage* is a layered birthday cake. **DELICIOUS**

laksetartar salmon tartar, served with sour cream and capers.

langtidsbraiseret svineskank braised pork shank. See page 55 for a recipe.

leverpostej liver pâté made from pork liver, possibly also with bacon and/or anchovies. Served warm or cold as a topping on *smørrebrød*. See recipe, page 49. **NATIONAL FAVORITE**

linse small tart with cream filling, similar to a German linzer torte. May also have fruit or jam filling. **GOOD CHOICE**

lufttørret skinke air-dried ham.

lørdagskylling tray of frozen "Saturday chicken" pieces ready to bake—a weekend convenience food.

POPULAR   **Madeira sild** herring marinated in Madeira.

makrel i tomat mackerel packed in a tomato sauce, garnished with a bit of mayonnaise and used as a topping on *smørrebrød*.

makroner macaroons made with almonds, not coconut.

HOLIDAY FAVORITE   **mandelgave** almond prize (often a marzipan pig) given to the person who finds the whole almond in the *ris á l'amande*. A Christmas tradition.

mandelkage almond cake.

mandelrand almond mousse.

marengs meringue cookies.

marmorkage marble cake.

Matjes sild very mild salt herring. Sometimes called soused herring, *Matjes sild* is made from young, immature fish.

EXTRAORDINARY   **mazarinkage** classic single-layer almond cake made with marzipan, sometimes topped with chocolate ganache. Also called simply *mazarin*. See recipe, page 65.

TASTY   **mazarintærte** sweet tart made with a shortbread crust and a marzipan filling, glazed in white or dark chocolate, and decorated with nuts or candied berries.

medalje two round shortbread cookies put together with a cream filling, topped with an icing glaze and a berry or a square of red currant jelly.

NATIONAL FAVORITE   **medisterpølse** spicy sausage made of coarsely ground pork and bacon. Served frilled with boiled potatoes, gravy, and pickled red cabbage. Also spelled as two words: *medister pølse*.

melboller flour dumplings used in chicken soup. These can be purchased premade in Denmark.

millionbøf a dish made from ground beef browned with onions, commonly served with mashed potatoes or rice. The name literally means "million beef," which may refer to the number of pieces of meat.

HEALTHY CHOICE   **mysli** muesli, a cereal made of oatmeal and dried fruit.

mælkeærter a Southern Jutland summer dish made from milk, carrots, cubed potatoes, and peas. Can be made thin as a soup or thick as a stew, and is served with smoked pork or ham. Also called *snysk*.

møllehjul a pull-apart "mill wheel" of separate wheat rolls baked together into large round.

GOOD CHOICE   **napoleonshatte** tri-cornered cookies made of shortcrust pastry, filled with marzipan, and with a layer of dark chocolate on the bottom. Named after Napoleon's hat, they probably date back to the latter half of the 1800s.

napoleonskage rectangular cream cake made up of two layers of puff pastry with raspberry jam, cake cream, and whipped cream in the center. This cake, named in Napoleon's honor, is glazed with white or brown glaze with rum flavoring. **DELICIOUS**

nougat nougat. French, or white, nougat is a hard or chewy candy made with sugar and/or honey and roasted nuts. Brown nougat also has cocoa butter and chocolate among its ingredients. Also see *blød nougat*. **VERY POPULAR**

nytårstorsk boiled cod with mustard sauce eaten on New Year's Eve.

oksehalesuppe oxtail soup or ragout.

oksekøds ragout beef stew. Ragout is a French term for a stew made of any type of meat.

oksesteg beef pot roast served with gravy, potatoes, and carrots— traditional *kromad* (inn food). Also called *gammeldags oksesteg*. **NATIONAL FAVORITE**

opbagt sovs sauce made from butter and flour (a béchamel sauce). Can also be made as a brown sauce or gravy.

ostebord assortment of cheese, cheese platter.

Othellokage cake with a macaroon or biscuit bottom layer, cake cream between the additional sponge layers, and a chocolate glaze on top edged with whipped cream. Created by La Glace Conditorie in Copenhagen in the 19th century in honor of a production of Shakespeare's Othello at The Royal Theater. Also called Othello *lagkage* (Othello layer cake). **EXTRAORDINARY**

overflødighedshorn cornucopia or horn of plenty made of *kransekage* (almond pastry cake) usually filled with chocolates or candies and used for birthdays. **ELEGANT**

pandekager crepe-like pancakes served for dessert with jam or sugar.

paneret rødspætterfilet med smørsovs breaded plaice fillet with butter sauce. **NATIONAL FAVORITE**

pariserbøf ground beef patties, flatter than *hakkebøf*, served with horseradish, copped, pickled beets, chopped raw onion, chopped pickles, capers, and egg yolk on toast (a lunch dish). Also spelled as two words, *pariser bøf*. **POPULAR**

parisertoast grilled ham and cheese sandwich.

pebernød spicy cookie shaped into a small ball. Although the name means peppernut, *pebbernødder* can be made with or **HOLIDAY FAVORITE**

without pepper. They date back to the Middle Ages, when they may have been made using *rugbrød* dough with spices added.

peberrodsovs creamed horseradish sauce.

persillesovs béchamel white sauce with lots of fresh parsley, served over boiled potatoes, and also slices of fried pork belly. See *stegt flæsk med persillesovs.*

pocherede æbler poached apples.

pocherede æg poached egg or eggs.

pomfritter French fries. Also called by their French name— *pommes frites*—or simply *fritter.*

DELICIOUS **pære belle Helene** poached pears served with vanilla ice cream and chocolate syrup. From the French, *poire belle Hélène.*

pølsebrød hot dog roll.

pølsemix mixed grill of sausages.

Påske lam Easter lamb. The traditional Easter meal is a large lunch (*koldt bord*), but some families eat lamb for dinner.

DELICIOUS **rabarbergrød** rhubarb compote thickened with potato flour and served with cream as a dessert.

rabarberkompot rhubarb conserves, boiled with sugar but not thickened. Served with chicken. See recipe, page 59.

EXCELLENT **rabarbertrifli** rhubarb trifle. See recipe, page 66.

rejecocktail shrimp cocktail.

rejesalat shrimp salad, often used as *pålæg.*

NATIONAL FAVORITE **remoulade** sauce made of mayonnaise, capers, pickles, and mustard, similar to tartar sauce. See recipe, page 58.

ribbensteg pork rib roast, usually cooked and served with the crackling on. This is one of three cuts of meat that can be used to make *flæskesteg.*

HOLIDAY FAVORITE **ris á l'amande** rich rice dish made by mixing cooled *risengrød* (rice pudding) with whipped cream, sugar, vanilla, and slivered almonds. Served on Christmas Eve with cherry sauce and a hidden single whole almond. The person who finds it gets a special gift (*mandelgave*). Named for the French *riz à l'amande*, rice with almonds. Also spelled *risalamande*. See recipe, page 64.

HOLIDAY FAVORITE **risengrød** unsweetened rice porridge, made by boiling rice with milk and salt. Served as a meal, or as a dessert topped with butter, sugar, and ground cinnamon. Traditionally eaten by *nisser* (elves) at Christmas. Risengrød serves as the base for *ris á l'amande.*

risklatter a type of "*klatkage*" using leftover *risengrød.*

roast bøf roast beef, sometimes referred to by its English name. If served cold on a *smørrebrød*, only cooked to rare.

romkugler rum balls: truffles made from leftover crumbled cookies, cake, or bread combined with cocoa, rum, and ground hazelnuts. Similar to *studenterbrød*.   POPULAR

rosinboller rolls with raisins.

roulade jelly roll of sponge cake with either jelly, whipped cream, or ice cream filling.   EXCELLENT

Rubensteinkage cream layer cake flavored with rum. This cake, which is decorated with miniature cream puffs, dark chocolate, crushed *nougat*, and whipped cream, is named for the pianist Anton Rubenstein.

rugbrødslagkage a layer cake from Southern Jutland made with small pieces of rye bread (*rugbrød*) with cocoa and almonds added, and whipped cream and jam between the layers.   REGIONAL SPECIALTY

rugkiks classic crisp rye cracker seasoned with caraway, which originated on the island of Bornholm.   REGIONAL SPECIALTY

rullepølse lunch meat made of dried lamb, pork, or veal seasoned with pepper and other spices, rolled up, and tied. After being cooked it is cooled in a special press. Served sliced on *rugbrød*.   POPULAR

rundstykker round breakfast rolls. A breakfast staple.   NATIONAL FAVORITE

rysteribs red currants sweetened with sugar. Literally means "shaken currants," as the berries are shaken with granulated sugar and then left to macerate for an hour or more. Served with rice pudding.

rævsovs mustard sauce served with marinated salmon and other fish dishes. Literally called "fox sauce," probably because of its reddish color. See recipe, page 44.

rød pølse a long, skinny, red pork hot dog sold in street stands.   NATIONAL FAVORITE

rødgrød med fløde red fruit pudding served with cream. See recipe, page 65.   NATIONAL FAVORITE

rødkål pickled red cabbage prepared with butter or duck fat, salt, vinegar, sugar or jelly, and spices. A popular everyday dish and garnish for *smørrebrød*, red cabbage is also traditionally served hot for Christmas, accompanying pork roast, duck, or goose. Also spelled as two words: *rød kål*. See recipe, page 59.   NATIONAL FAVORITE

rødspættefilet, paneret breaded and fried fillet of plaice. Served with *remoulade* or parsley sauce.

røget hellefisk smoked halibut.

røget laks cold smoked salmon. Smoking at a cool temperature (around 99°F) does not cook the salmon, preserving its delicate texture. *Hjemrøget laks* are smoked at home on top of the stove.

Røget laks is served on *smørrebrød* topped with small shrimp, lemon, and dill or *æggestand* (scrambled egg).

NATIONAL FAVORITE **røget ål med røræg** smoked eel, served on an open-faced sandwich with *æggestand* (scrambled egg).

røræg scrambled egg.

råcreme custard made of raw egg yolk, sugar, and whipping cream.

Rådhuspandekager crepes with cream filling and apricot jam. Developed in the late 1930s, these were originally only served at the Copenhagen Town Hall (the name means "Town Hall Pancakes") or at official city events. To celebrate Copenhagen's 800th anniversary in 1967, a record-breaking 70,000 servings were handed out on the walking street Strøget. Using 150 standard-size crepe pans it took 14 days to make them all.

REGIONAL SPECIALTY **sakkuk** boiled barley pudding, a Fanø specialty.

saltkød thin-sliced salted beef used as a topping for *smørrebrød*.

sandkage pound cake made with butter (as opposed to the traditional layer cake, which is does not include butter). The name literally means "sand cake."

ELEGANT **Sarah Bernhardt kage** small cake named for the French actress. An almond macaroon base is topped with a truffle-like chocolate filling and covered in melted chocolate.

sildebord Bornholm buffet of mostly herring dishes.

REGIONAL SPECIALTY **Skagen sild** marinated herring mixed with apples, shallots, sour cream, and dill, a specialty from the tip of the Jutland peninsula.

skidne æg "messy eggs"—hard-boiled eggs with a slightly soft yolk, served in a mustard sauce.

skimmelost moldy cheese.

DELICIOUS **skinkesalat** ham salad made with chopped ham and mayonnaise, chopped onion, and chives. Used as *pålæg*.

NATIONAL FAVORITE **skipperlabskovs** sailors' stew made of cubed beef or pork, onion, and potatoes cooked to a hash-like consistency. Also called *labskovs*. See recipe, page 54.

Skærtorsdagskål cabbage dish served on Maundy Thursday comprised of different types of cabbage cooked with pork and other meats.

smushi a recent fusion food that combines the concepts of sushi and *smørrebrød* to make artistic miniature open-faced sandwiches.

DELICIOUS **smørbirkes** rolls with poppy seeds.

smørkage a pastry. See *Dagmartærte*.

smørrebrød open-faced sandwiches. The word literally translates to "buttered bread." NATIONAL FAVORITE

snapsemad an open-face sandwich with herring and potatoes. The name means "food to go with *snaps*."

snegl spiral pastry or sticky bun, sometimes with chocolate on top. The name means "snail." See also *kanelsnegl*. GOOD CHOICE

snobrød bread cooked over a campfire by taking white bread dough and twisting it around a stick.

snysk milk-based vegetable soup. See *mælkeærter*.

sodavandsis Popsicle-like treats.

softis soft ice cream. POPULAR

Sol over Gudhjem open-faced sandwich featuring smoked herring, served with sliced radish, chives, and an egg yolk on *rugbrød*. A specialty from the island of Bornholm, the name literally means "Sun over (the town of) Gudhjem." REGIONAL SPECIALTY

solæg pickled hard-boiled eggs used in the sun egg ceremony. A specialty of southern Jutland. REGIONAL SPECIALTY

sommersalat chopped radishes, cucumbers, and chives in a dressing made from *ymer* and/or crème fraîche and *rygeost*.

souper an old-fashioned term for a late supper at a party or reception. Sometimes seen with French spelling: *soupé*.

spandauer round Danish pastry with jam or an egg cream filling in a depression in the center. Nicknamed "the baker's bad eye," although you should not order it in a bakery by that name. NATIONAL FAVORITE

specie round cookie made of flour, sugar, butter, and sometimes almonds. *Specier* can also be made with chocolate or lemon.

spegepølse summer sausage sometimes now known as salami— can be made from a variety of meats including pork and beef. Sliced as *pålæg*. NATIONAL FAVORITE

spegesild salted marinated herring. NATIONAL FAVORITE

spejderhagl big balls of strong licorice; means "Boy Scout hail."

spejlæg fried egg.

sportskage Conditoriet La Glace cake made of crushed nougat, whipped cream, a macaroon bottom, and caramelized choux pastry. Although the name means "sports cake," it was actually named for the play "Sports Man" rather than any athletic event.

sprødt svær crispy pork rind. DELICIOUS

stegt and med svesker og æbler roast duck stuffed with prunes and apples.

stegt flæsk med persillesovs slices of fried pork belly served with potatoes and parsley sauce. NATIONAL FAVORITE

stegt gås roast goose, a traditional Danish Christmas dish.

stegt kylling roast chicken.

NATIONAL FAVORITE **stegt rødspætte med persillesauce** fried plaice fillet served with a parsley sauce.

stegt torsk med remoulade fried cod with *remoulade* sauce.

EXTRAORDINARY **stegt ål** fried eel. It is the tradition that everyone eats so much that the bones form a circle around the rim of the plate.

stegte sild i eddike fried herring in a vinegar and sugar solution, served with sliced raw onions on top of *rugbrød*.

stenbiderrogn lumpfish eggs (caviar). A Swedish dish popular in Denmark, using eggs from the lumpfish (*Cyclopterus lumpus*) served on toast or blinis with crème fraîche and raw onions.

NATIONAL FAVORITE **stjerneskud** literally, "shooting star"—a popular *smørrebrød* which, on a base of toasted white bread, features a piece of steamed fillet of plaice and a piece of fried fillet of plaice, topped with shrimp, mayonnaise, caviar, and lemon. See recipe, page 50.

studenterbrød inexpensive, dense bars supposedly made from leftover cake and pastries, with rum flavor added. The name means "student bread." Similar to *romkugler* (rum balls).

REGIONAL SPECIALTY **stuvet hvidkål** cabbage served in a thick béchamel sauce, sometime served with cinnamon sugar on top. A Jutland favorite.

stuvede, flødestuvede kartofler potatoes served in a thick béchamel sauce.

stuvede ærter peas served in a thick béchamel sauce.

sukkerbrunede kartofler caramelized potatoes. See *brunede kartofler*.

REGIONAL SPECIALTY **surrib** pork boiled with vinegar and spices, then cooled in an aspic. Eaten sliced with *rugbrød* and strong mustard. A traditional Southern Jutland specialty, especially at Christmas.

Svensk pølseret potato and sausage stew. Although the name means "Swedish hot dog dish," this stew is actually Danish.

svinekød i karry pork in curry sauce.

NATIOINAL FAVORITE **svinemørbrad med æbler og svesker** pork tenderloin cooked with apples and prunes.

sylte headcheese traditionally made of a pig's head, but now made with pork and veal shoulder. The meat is boiled and then taken off the bone, layered with spices, and pressed. Served sliced with picked beets and mustard.

syv slags grønt literally, "seven types of green," a vegetable soup served on Maundy Thursday.

sødsuppe fruit soup made of apples, peaches, plums, or other fruits and berries and thickened with tapioca or gelatin. The name means "sweet soup." Served hot or cold.

tartar beef tartare (raw ground or scraped beef) served on *rugbrød,*   ELEGANT
topped with onions, grated horseradish, and a raw egg yolk.

tarteletter tartlets with filling such as boiled chicken, with   POPULAR
asparagus, carrots, or peas, in a béchamel cream sauce. Can also
be filled with fish, ham, or shrimp. Premade shells are available
in the grocery store in Denmark.

teboller slightly sweet "tea rolls," sometimes made with cardamom
and raisins.

thebirkes flaky morning pastry with a thin layer of marzipan   DELICIOUS
inside, topped with poppy seeds. Also called simply *birkes.*

Tivoli kage round pastry topped with white marzipan and red swirls.

tomatsild marinated herring in tomato sauce.

trifli trifle.

træstammer tree-trunk shaped pastries dipped in chocolate.   POPULAR

tvebakker rusks, small toasted unsweetened biscuits eaten in soup   NATIONAL FAVORITE
or buttered as a snack.

tørkage small cake or pastry, such as a Napoleon's hat, without a
whipped cream filling. The name means "dry cake."

tørrede dabs dried, salted dabs or other flat fish such as plaice.   REGIONAL SPECIALTY
Traditionally the fish is boiled and served over mashed potatoes,
topped with fried onions, smoked pork cubes, and the fat from
frying the onions and pork. Other names for the dish are *tørrede
isinger* and *tørrede jyder,* which literally means "dried Jutlanders."

vandbakkelse cream puff, profiterole, or éclair.   DELICIOUS

vandgrød barley porridge made with water.

vaniljekranse vanilla cookie shaped like a wreath. These traditional   HOLIDAY FAVORITE
cookies date to the 1840s. See recipe, page 67.

varme hveder cardamom rolls eaten on the eve of *Store Bededag*
(Great Prayer Day). See *hvedeknopper.*

varmrøget laks brined salmon smoked over heat.

vinsuppe wine soup. A southern Jutland porridge made of whole   REGIONAL SPECIALTY
barley groats, prunes, and a bit of wine. Served with ham.

wienerbrød literally, "Viennese bread," this pastry is called   NATIONAL FAVORITE
"Danish" in other parts of the world. Multiple thin layers of
dough are folded over with margarine or butter and then filled
with marzipan and garnished with almonds and sugar. The term
wienerbrød is also used to describe a class of pastries that

includes *smørkage*, *Dagmartærte*, and kringle, which is a large *wienerbrød* in the shape of a pretzel.

POPULAR **wienerkage** Vienna cake or Vienna tart (*wienertærte*). Originally a torte with many layers, this traditional cake always features a layer of raspberry jam.

wienerpølse a boiled hot dog.

EXCELLENT **æbleflæsk** traditional dish of fried pork slices or bacon served with a compote of apples and onions. The name means "apple pork."

æblegrød apple pudding.

æblekage apple charlotte or pudding, made of layers of stewed apples, bread crumbs, and whipped cream. Also called *bondepige med slør*, which means "veiled farm girl." *Æblekage* means apple cake, but this isn't really a cake. Also called *gammeldags æblekage*. See recipe, page 62.

NATIONAL FAVORITE **æbleskiver** round Danish "doughnuts" made with a pancake-like batter and cooked on the stovetop in a special pan. Traditionally filled with apple slices, although there are many other variations. See recipe, page 61.

æblesnitter turnover with apple and nuts.

æggekage an omelet served with tomato, bacon, and sometimes also fried pork rind. See recipe, page 53.

HEALTHY CHOICE **æggemad** a *smørrebrød* made with slices of hardboiled egg.

æggesalat egg salad.

æggesnaps dessert made with eggs and sugar. Although the name of this dish means "egg *snaps*," there is no alcohol in it. Raw egg yolks and sugar (and optionally a bit of cocoa powder) are whisked together to make this sweet, rich childhood favorite. Also used as a topping, for example on *øllebrød*.

æggestand scrambled eggs, cooked in a water bath (not on a griddle or frying pan), and used sliced as a garnish on *smørrebrød*.

NATIONAL FAVORITE **øllebrød** porridge made from beer and *rugbrød*, served with heavy cream or milk. Sometimes *æggesnaps* (raw egg yolk mixed with sugar) or cream is used to make a pattern on the top. An easy supper or breakfast dish that was once a common dish.

Foods & Flavors Guide

This chapter is a comprehensive list of foods, spices, kitchen utensils and cooking terms in Danish, with English translations. As you are looking for a word, remember that there are three letters that come after Z in the Danish alphabet: æ, ø, and å. Please review the additional information in the *Menu Guide* (p. 83) for help in understanding alternative endings on Danish words. Danish recipes are in metrics, and most foods are sold by the kilo. You will find sentences that will help you shop in a Danish market in the *Helpful Phrases* chapter on page 79.

A38 a fresh, slightly soured milk product used on cereal, in smoothies, and in dressings.

aborre European perch, a freshwater fish of the family Percidae (*Perca fluviatilis*).

abrikos apricot.

ad libitum can refer to either all-you-can eat, or eating until satiated. This Latin phrase literally means "in accordance with desire" and is where the term "ad lib" comes from.

aftenkaffe evening coffee, often served after dinner and enjoyed with chocolates and pastries.

aftensmad dinner; literally, "evening meal." Also called *middag*, which means middle of the day and refers back to when the biggest meal of the day was at noon.

agerhøne partridge. The plural of *agerhøne* is *agerhøns*.

agurk English cucumber used to make cucumber salad, a popular side dish. Pickling cucumbers are called *asier*.

ahornsirup maple syrup.

akvavit aquavit ("the water of life"), another name for *snaps*.

alkoholfri non-alcoholic.

allehånde allspice.

almindelig common, everyday. Sometimes abbreviated as *alm*.

ananas pineapple.

and duck. The plural of *and* is *ænder*.

andefedt duck fat.

andesteg roast duck.

anis anise.

anretning platter, as in *fiskeanretning*, which means fish platter. The word *ret* refers to a course, such as *forret* (appetizer) and *hovedret* (main course).

ansjos anchovy.

appelsin orange, the fruit. The Danish word for the color is *orange*.

appelsinjuice orange juice.

appetitvækker appetizer.

artiskok artichoke. The Jerusalem artichoke is *jordskok*.

asie a special pickling cucumber, *Cucumis sativus*, and the pickles made from it.

asparges asparagus, a popular springtime delicacy. *Grøn asparges* is green; *hvid asparges* is white.

aubergine eggplant.

babyspinat baby spinach.

bacon bacon.

bagekartoffel baking potato.

bagepulver baking powder.

bager baker.

bageri bakery.

bagning baking.

bagt baked.

bagværk baked goods.

banan banana.

bankekød beef stew meat.

basilikum basil.

batat sweet potato. Another word for sweet potato is *sødkartoffel*.

bedst best.

belagt covered.

ben leg, leg bone. Another word for bone is *knogle*.

benløs deboned, boneless.

besk bitter.

bestik silverware, flatware.

birkes poppy seeds. Also a breakfast roll topped with poppy seeds that is sometimes called *thebirkes*.

bitter bitter. Also refers to bitters, an aromatic alcoholic drink.

bjesk *snaps* (aquavit) made slightly bitter with an extract of wormwood.

bjorr strong liquor from the Viking Age made from fermented apple cider.

bladselleri celery. Celeriac is *knoldselleri* or simply *selleri*.

blandet mixed, blended.

blod blood.

blodappelsin blood orange.

blomkål cauliflower.

blomme plum.

blomsterknop flower bud. Some flower buds, such as those from *ramsløg* (wild garlic), are edible.

blæksprutte squid, octopus, or cuttlefish, mollusks in the class Cephalopoda. The name literally means "ink squirter."

blød soft, softened.

blå blue.

blå Bornholmer blue cheese from Bornholm.

blåbær blueberry or blueberries.

blåmusling blue mussel.

blåskimmel ost generic name for all blue cheeses, including Danablu, Stilton, and Roquefort. *Blåskimmel* literally means "blue mold."

boghvede buckwheat. *Boghvedemel* is buckwheat flour.

bolcher sweets, hard candies.

boller rolls or balls. See also *kødboller* and *fiskeboller* in the *Menu Guide*.

bonde farmer, peasant.

bord table.

bordbestilling table reservation.

boysenbær boysenberry or boysenberries.

brazen bream (*Abramis brama*).

bredbladet persille flat-leaf parsley.

brissel thymus from veal or lamb. The plural of *brissel* is *brisler*.

brokkoli broccoli. Sometimes called by its English name.

brombær blackberry or blackberries.

brosme tusk (*Brosme brosme*), a cod-like fish in the ling family, Lotidae. Tusk (or cusk) is abundant around Iceland and the Faroe Islands.

brun brown.

brun farin soft brown sugar.

brunch brunch.

brune ris brown rice.

brunet browned, caramelized.

brus fizz.

bryggeri brewery.

bryst breast.

brændenælder stinging nettles (*Urtica dioica*). This nutritious herbaceous perennial must be soaked in water or cooked to remove the stinging chemicals from the hairs before using.

brændevin *snaps* (aquavit), vodka, and other strong spirits.

brændt burned.

brød bread. Danes traditionally eat more rye bread (*rugbrød*) than white bread (*franskbrød*).

brødskive slice of bread.

brøndkarse watercress.

budding pudding.

butterdej puff pastry; *pâte feuilletée*.

bydes til is offered as an accompaniment, as in "rum is offered with this dish."

byg barley.

byggryn barley groats.

bæger dish for serving ice cream, as an alternative to a cone.

bækørred brook trout (*Salmo trutta fario*).

bælgfrugter legumes.

bær berry or berries.

bøf steak.

bøgehat woodland mushroom (*Hypsizygus tessellatus*).

bøgeskud spring beech leaves (literally, "shoots").

bønner beans.

bønnespirer bean sprouts.

børnemenu children's menu.

cashewnød cashew.

champignon mushroom.

chef manager or director. The term is now sometimes used to mean chef. See also *kok*.

Cherry Heering liqueur flavored with black cherries. Named for Danish distillery owner Peter Heering. It is used in cocktails such as the Singapore Sling and is sometimes misspelled as *Cherry Herring*.

chilipeber chile pepper.

chokolade chocolate.

cidereddike cider vinegar. Another word for cider vinegar is *æbleeddike*, which means "apple vinegar."

citron lemon.

citrusfrugt citrus fruit.

courgette zucchini. Also called by its English name.

Crema Dania rich double-cream Danish cheese with an edible rind and soft interior. Also called Crema Danica.

creme custard or filling.

cremefraiche sour cream that is less sour and often higher in fat content than American sour cream. Available in a variety of fat content levels ranging from 9 to 36 percent. Also referred to with the French *crème fraîche*.

daddel date. The plural of *daddel* is *dadler*.

dagens suppe soup of the day.

dampet steamed.

Danablu trade name for Danish blue cheese. Made from cow's milk cheese aged with rods treated with the mold *Penicillium roqueforti*, which is thereby distributed throughout the formed curds.

Danbo popular semi-soft aged cow's milk cheese. Gamle Ole is a pungent Danbo, and Kong Christian is a Danbo with caraway seeds added.

dansk Danish.

dej dough.

delicat exquisite, savory.

dessert dessert.

dessert surprice surprise dessert, chef's choice.

dild dill.

diverse various.

dressing salad dressing.

drik beverage. Also called *drikkelse*.

drikkepenge tip, gratuity.

drink a drink.

druer grapes. Another word for grapes is *vindruer*.

drys sprinkles.

drøj robust.

ds. abbreviation for *dåse* (can).

due pigeon.

dybfrossen frozen.

dyrefilet fillet of venison.

dyrekølle haunch of venison.

dyrevildt game.

dådyr specific type of venison (*Dama dama*).

dåse tin, can. Abbreviated *ds*.

dåsemad canned food.

dåseåbner can opener.

eddike vinegar.

eftermiddagskaffe afternoon coffee break.

efterår autumn.

elg moose. Not native to Denmark, unless there is a harsh winter and they swim over from Sweden.

emhætte stove hood.

enebær juniper berry or juniper berries.

Esrom strong, aromatic semi-soft cow's milk cheese named after Esrum Kloster (abbey) near Hillerød. Esrom is a Port Salut cheese considered to be one of the world's top "stinky" (or well-aged) cheeses.

estragon tarragon.

fad dish or pot.

fadøl draught or tap beer.

farmors paternal grandmother's—a recipe that comes from *farmor*, for example. (Something from a maternal grandmother is *mormors*.)

farseret stuffed, as in cabbage stuffed with forcemeat.

fasan pheasant.

fastost firm cheese.

fattigmands poor man's (adjective). Also a deep-fried cookie.

fedt fat, including pork fat sometimes used as a spread.

feinschmecker German term meaning gourmand or epicurian.

feldsalat corn salad (*Valerianella*), a leaf vegetable used as a salad green.

fennikel fennel.

fersk fresh.

fersken peach.

ferskvandsfisk freshwater fish.

figen fig. The plural of *figen* is *figner*.

filodej phyllo dough.

finthakket finely chopped.

fisk fish.

fiskeanretning fish platter.

fjerkræ poultry.

fjordrejer small shrimp found in saltwater fjords. Common shrimp are called simply *rejer*.

fjæsing greater weever, a marine fish (*Trachinus draco*) served smoked. This fish has highly poisonous dorsal spines that are dangerous to step on.

flad flat.

flaske bottle.

flaskeøl bottled beer.

flormelis confectioner's sugar or icing sugar: powdered sugar with a small amount of potato starch added to prevent clumping. Also called *florsukker*. *Melis* is an antiquated term for cane sugar.

flækærter split peas, usually yellow peas (*gule ærter*).

flæsk pork.

flæskesteg pork roast served with pork rind crackling.

flæskesvær pork rind crackling. Also called simply *svær*.

fløde cream.

flødeglasur frosting or glaze made with cream cheese.

flødeis ice cream.

flødekaramel caramel, toffee.

flødeost cream cheese.

flødeskum whipped cream, which is served unsweetened in Denmark. Also called *pisket fløde*.

forel rainbow trout (*Oncorhynchus mykiss*). Also called *regnbueørred*.

forkortelser abbreviations.

formfranskbrød white bread shaped in a sandwich loaf. Also called *franskbrød*.

forret appetizer, first course.

forvarm preheat.

forår spring.

forårsløg spring onions.

franskbrød white bread, either traditional French bread or white bread shaped in a sandwich loaf (which is also called *formfranskbrød*).

franskvaffel filled cookie.

fremgangsmåde procedure (in a recipe).

friland free range.

frisk fresh.

friskbagt freshly baked.

friskplukket freshly picked.

frokost lunch.

fromage mousse.

frossen frozen.

frugt fruit

frø a seed (*et frø*) or seeds. Also means a frog (*en frø*).

fuld drunk. The Danish word for "full" is *mæt*.

fuldkornsbrød whole-grain bread.

fyld filling.

fyldt filled or stuffed.

Fynbo semi-hard cow's milk cheese from the island of *Fyn* (Funen). Fynbo is a mild cheese with a taste influenced by the buckwheat grown on *Fyn*.

fælleshave community garden.

færdig finished.

færdigmad meals to go, ready-made dish. Also called *færdigret*.

får sheep.

gaffel fork.

gammel old.

Gammel Dansk a bitters liquor made using many different herbs and spices. The name literally means "Old Danish."

gammeldags old-fashioned. Sometimes abbreviated as *gl. dags*.

garniture garnish, side dish.

ged goat.

gedde pike (*Esox lucius*).

gedeost goat cheese.

gelé jelly.

geranium flowering herb wild geranium (*Geranium maculatum*). Also called *storkenæb* (cranesbill).

glas drinking glass. Also the material glass.

glaseret glazed.

glasur icing, frosting.

glutenfri gluten-free.

godter assorted candies, sweet tidbits.

granatæble pomegranate.

grapefrugt grapefruit.

gratin oven dish topped with bread crumbs and/or cheese; au gratin.

grill grill.

gris pig, pork.

grov coarse.

grovbrød coarse whole-grain bread.

grundsovs basic gravy.

græsk yoghurt Greek yogurt.

græskar pumpkin, squash.

græskarkærneolie pumpkin seed oil.

grød porridge, pudding.

grødris short-grain rice used to make rice pudding.

grøn the color green. Plural adjective is *grønne*, as in *grønne bønner*.

grønkål curly kale (*Brassica oleracea acephala*).

grønne bønner green beans.

grønsager vegetables. Also spelled *grøntsager*.

grønthandler greengrocer, a shop selling fruits and vegetables.

grøntsagsbouillon vegetable stock.

guf fluffy marshmallow sauce used as a topping on ice cream cones. *Guf* is also a generic term for candy.

gule ærter yellow peas; also a thick soup made with yellow peas. Also called *flækærter*, which means "split peas."

gulerod carrot. The plural of *gulerod* is *gulerødder*.

gurkemeje turmeric.

gylden golden.

gær yeast.

gås goose.

hakkekød ground beef. Also called *hakket kalvekød*.

hakket ground or chopped.

halv half.

hane cock, a male chicken.

hare hare.

hasselnød hazelnut.

havaborre European seabass (*Dicentrarchus labrax*).

Havarti buttery, sweet, semi-soft cow's milk cheese named after a farm called Havartigård north of Copenhagen.

havbras gilt-head seabream (*Sparus aurata*).

havkat catfish (*Anarhichas lupus*). Another name for *havkat* is *koteletfisk*.

havregryn rolled oats.

havsalt sea salt.

havtaske angler fish, a type of monkfish (*Lophius piscatorius*).

havtorn sea-buckthorn berries (*Hippophae rhamnoides*). These berries come from deciduous shrubs that grow in Danish coastal areas, and although acidic and unpleasant to eat raw, they are very high in vitamin C.

havørred brown trout (*Salmo trutta trutta*).

hedvin wine fortified with brandy, sherry, or other distilled beverage; *vin fortifié*. The term is used to describe drinks such as sherry and Port that have an alcoholic content higher than wine but lower than aquavit.

hellefisk Greenland halibut or turbot (*Reinhardtius hippoglossoides*), often served smoked.

helleflynder Atlantic halibut (*Hippoglossus hippoglossus*).

hel whole.

hestebønner fava or broad beans. Literally, "horse beans" (*Vicia faba*).

hindbær raspberry or raspberries.

hirse millet.

hjemmebagt home baked.

hjemmelavet homemade.

hjerte heart.

hjortefilet venison fillet.

hjortetaksalt hartshorn salt. Called ammonium carbonate in Canada and the US, it is available in some drugstores.

honning honey.

honningmelon honeydew melon.

hornfisk garfish or needlefish (*Belone belone*).

hovedret main course.

hovedsalat head of lettuce. Also called *salathoved*.

humle hops (*Humulus lupulus*).

hummer lobster. The common European lobster (*Homarus gammarus*) is much larger than the *jomfruhummer*, or Norway lobster (*Nephrops norvegicus*).

husblas gelatin.

husets of the house, as in "the specialty of the house."

husmandsasparges silver beet foliage (*Beta vulgaris* var. *Vulgaris*), which is related to chard. *Husmandsaspareges* literally means, "poor man's asparagus." Also called *sølvbede* or *bladbede*.

hval whale.

hvede wheat.

hvedemel wheat flour.

hvedekim wheat germ.

hvedeklid wheat bran.

hvid white.

hvidkål round green cabbage, although the Danish name literally means "white cabbage" (*Brassica oleracea capitata*). The Danes also eat pointed cabbage (oxheart) and red cabbage.

hvidløg garlic.

hvidtøl malt beer.

hvidvin white wine.

hvilling fish commonly known as whiting (*Merlangius merlangius*).

hyben rosehips from wild roses (*Rosa rugosa*).

hygge a verb and noun relating to the particularly Danish concept of being "cozy." The adjective describing this state is *hyggelig*.

hyldeblomst elder flower (*Sambucus nigra*).

hyldeblomstsaft elder flower extract, served mixed with plain or sparkling water. Also served mixed with white wine as a St. Hans Evening cordial.

hyldebær elderberry or elderberries.

hytteost cottage cheese.

højtbelagt piled high, usually in reference to *smørrebrød* (see *Menu Guide*).

høne hen. The plural of *høne* is *høns*.

hønsebouillon chicken bouillon.

hørfrø flaxseed, linseed.

hørfrøolie linseed oil.

høst harvest.

høvlet grated.

håndplukket hand picked.

hårdkogt æg hard-boiled egg.

i aspic in aspic.

i cocotte in a small lidded pot.

i vin in wine.

indmad entrails.

ingefær ginger.

inklusiv including. Abbreviated as *inkl.*

is ice cream or ice.

ishus ice cream stand. Also called *iskiosk*.

ising a flat fish known as the common dab (*Limanda limanda*). *Ising* (also spelled *issing*) is used in the Fanø specialty *bakskuld* and in the Northern Jutland specialty *tørrede dabs* (see *Menu Guide*).

iskiosk ice cream stand. Also called *ishus*.

ispind Popsicle-like ice cream treat on a stick.

iste iced tea.

isvaffel ice cream cone.

jagt hunt.

jomfruhummer Norway lobster or langoustine (*Nephrops norvegicus*), which is smaller than the common European lobster, which is called simply *hummer*. *Jomfruhummer* means "maiden lobster," although they are of course not all female.

jordbær strawberry or strawberries.

jordnød peanut. Also called by the English name.

jordnøddesmør peanut butter.

jordskok Jerusalem artichoke.

juice juice.

jul Christmas. *Jule* is the adjective referring to Christmas.

julebryg sweet, strong beer brewed at Christmas.

julefrokost Christmas lunch, often a *koldt bord* (buffet).

julesalat Belgian endive, grown by allowing chicory root to sprout in a dark place. The name means "Christmas lettuce."

jævning roux; thickening for gravy (usually flour and water).

kaffe coffee.

kaffebord an array of baked goods served with coffee. Literally, "coffee table."

kaffepause morning coffee break.

kage cake.

kagecreme custard.

kakao cocoa.

kakaomælk chocolate milk.

kalkun turkey.

kalv calf, veal.

kalvebryst breast of veal.

kamillete chamomile tea.

kammuslinger scallops.

kandis hard candy, usually crystalized rock sugar.

kanel cinnamon.

kanelsukker cinnamon sugar.

kanin rabbit.

kantarel chanterelle mushroom (*Cantharellus cibarius*).

kapers capers, the unripened flower buds of *Capparis spinosa*.

karamel caramel.

kardemomme cardamom.

Karl Johan svamp penny bun mushroom (*Boletus edulis*), named after the French-born Swedish King Charles XIV John.

karpefisk carp (*Cyprinus carpio*).

karry curry.

karse garden cress.

kartoffel potato. The plural of *kartoffel* is *kartofler*.

kartoffelmel potato flour.

kastanje chestnut.

kejserhat king trumpet mushroom, a type of oyster mushroom (*Pleurotus eryngii*). The name means "emperor's hat."

kerner seeds or pits.

ketchup ketchup, catsup.

kidneybønner kidney beans.

kiks sweet crackers or cookies (in England, biscuits).

kikærter chickpeas, garbanzo beans.

kildevand spring water. *Kildevand* is offered *med brus*, carbonated or sparkling, or *uden brus*, still or without carbonation.

kildeørred brook trout (*Salvelinus fontinalis*).

kinakål Chinese cabbage, bok choy.

kirsebær cherry or cherries.

kiwi kiwi.

klar clear, as in clear soup.

klipfisk salted and dried fish, usually cod.

knasende crunchy.

kniv knife.

knivspids a pinch, literally, "a knifepoint's worth." Abbreviated *knsp*.

knogle bone. Another word for (leg) bone is *ben*.

knoldselleri celery root, celeriac. Also called simply *selleri*. Celery is *bladselleri*.

knsp. abbreviation for *knivspids*—a pinch.

knudekål kohlrabi, turnip kale, cabbage turnip (*Brassica oleracea Acephala*).

knurhane bottom-living saltwater fish: red (*rød*) gurnard (*Eutrigla gurnardu*) or gray (*grå*) gurnard (*Trigla lucerna*).

knust crushed.

knækbrød crispbread, such as Swedish Wasa bread.

ko cow.

kogebog cookbook.

kogt boiled.

kok cook, chef.

kokos coconut.

kokosmakron coconut macaroon.

kold cold.

koldpresset rapsolie cold-pressed rapeseed oil.

kolonihave allotment garden.

kommen caraway. Not to be confused with cumin, which is *spidskommen*.

kompot stewed fruit, compote.

konditor pastry chef.

konditori fancy cake and pastry bakery.

konfekt chocolate candy.

kongekrabbe king crab (*Paralithodes camtschaticus*).

kop cup.

koriander coriander.

korn grain (see *majs* for corn on the cob).

kotelet cutlet.

koteletfisk catfish (*Anarhichas lupus*). Another name for *koteletfisk* is *havkat*.

krabbe crab.

krebs crayfish (*Astacus astacus*).

kromad the type of food traditionally served in Danish inns.

krondild dill that has been harvested after blossoming.

kruspersille parsley.

kryddereddike aromatic vinegar.

krydderi spices, seasoning.

kryddersnaps *snaps* (aquavit) that has been flavored with herbs or berries.

krydderurter herbs.

krydret spicy.

krymmel sprinkles, nonpareils, and other edible decorations for cakes or ice cream. See also *drys*.

kugle ball or scoop (of ice cream).

kuller haddock (*Melanogrammus aeglefinus*).

kulmule hake (*Merluccius merluccius*).

kulør food coloring; also called *madkulør*. *Brun kulør* is brown and is used to make *brun sovs* gravy (similar to Kitchen Bouquet Browning Sauce).

kumquat kumquat.

kuvert a place setting. The word literally means "envelope."

kvan angelica, a biennial plant known for its sweetly scented edible stems and roots (*Angelica archangelica*).

kvark soft, creamy, low-fat curd cheese used as a baking ingredient or spread. Also spelled *quark*.

kvæde quince (*Cydonia oblonga*).

kylling chicken.

kyllingebryst chicken breast.

kærnemælk buttermilk.

kød meat.

kødretter meat dishes.

køkken kitchen.

køleskab refrigerator.

kørvel chervil.

kål cabbage. Also the name for curly kale.

kålrabi kohlrabi.

kålroe rutabaga or Swedish turnip (*Brassica napobrassica*). May also be called simply *roe*.

lag på lag layered. Literally means "layer on layer."

lagkagebunde pre-made layers for layer cakes.

lakrids licorice.

laks Atlantic salmon, lox (*Salmo salar*).

lakseørred sea trout (*Salmo trutta*).

lam lamb.

lammebov shoulder of lamb.

lammekølle leg of lamb.

lange ling, or common ling, a fish in the cod family (*Molva molva*).

languster spiny lobsters, crayfish (*Palinurus vulgaris*).

laurbærblad bay leaf.

let light, low-fat.

letmælk low-fat milk. Skim milk is *minimælk* or *skummetmælk*.

lever liver.

lidt af hvert a sampling, a little bit of everything.

likør liqueur.

lille little or small. When referring to multiple objects the adjective is *små*.

lime lime.

linser lentils. *Linser* is also the plural of the small tart called a *linse*.

livret favorite dish. Literally means "life dish."

lokal local.

lugt smell.

lun warm.

lyssej pollock, which is also called light coalfish, or saithe (*Pollachius pollachius*). See *sej*.

lægge i blød soak to soften.

lækker delicious.

lækkeri delicacy.

lækkersulten hungry for a snack or something sweet.

løg onion.

løvstikke lovage (*Levisticum officinale*), a perennial whose leaves are used as an herb, roots as a vegetable, and seeds as a spice.

lår thigh.

mad food, meal.

Madeirasky or sovs *gelée* or gravy made with Madeira wine.

madkulør food coloring. Also called simply *kulør*.

madlavning cooking.

madolie vegetable oil.

madpakke packed lunch; brown bag lunch.

madæble cooking apple.

Maggiterninger Maggi brand bouillon cube.

majroe turnip.

majs corn.

makrel mackerel (*Scomber scombrus*).

makronbund macaroon base for a torte, made using marzipan or almonds, sugar, and egg whites (not coconut macaroon). Also called *makronlag*.

maltøl malt beer.

malurt wormwood.

mandel almond. The plural of *mandel* is *mandler*.

marcipan marzipan.

margarine margarine.

Maribo semi-hard cheese made from cow's milk, named for the town of Maribo on the island of Lolland. Maribo resembles Gouda, and the strength of the taste depends on how long it is aged.

marineret marinated.

marmelade marmalade, jam.

marv marrow.

mayonnaise mayonnaise. Also called simply *mayo*.

med with.

med brus carbonated; with bubbles.

med tilbehør includes accompanying side dishes.

medbragt mad food brought from home.

mejeri milk processor, dairy.

mejeriprodukter dairy products.

mel flour.

melasse molasses

melon melon.

melryster shaker for combining water and flour to make a roux to thicken gravy. Also called a *meljævner*.

menu prix fixe meal, or a menu.

menukort menu. Also called a *spisekort*.

mere more.

merian marjoram.

middag dinner or evening meal (although the word literally means "middle of the day").

mild mild.

mindre less.

minimælk skim or fat-free milk. Also called *skummetmælk*. Lowfat milk (1.5 to 1.8 percent milkfat) is *letmælk*.

minut minute.

mirabel small, European cherry plum (*Prunus cerasifera*).

mjød mead, an alcoholic beverage produced by fermenting honey and water.

moden ripe.

modnet aged.

Molbo delicate, light-flavored, semi-hard cow's milk cheese from Mols, the part of Jutland often referred to as its "nose."

moms sales tax.

morgenkaffe morning coffee; coffee break.

morgenmad breakfast.

mormormad grandmother's dish. Refers to traditional, old-fashioned food. *Mormor* means maternal grandmother—literally, "mother's mother."

mormors køkken grandmother's kitchen. Refers to traditional or old-fashioned foodways.

most cider (non-alcoholic).

multe mullet (*Mugilidae*).

multebær cloudberry or cloudberries (*Rubus chamaemorus*).

muskat nutmeg.

muslinger mussels.

mynte mint.

mælk milk.

mæt full, unable to eat more.

mør soft, tender.

mørbrad tenderloin, usually pork. Pork tenderloin is also called *svinemørbrad*.

mørbradbøf medallions of pork tenderloin.

mørdej shortcrust pastry; *pâte brisée*.

mørk dark.

mørksej pollock, saithe, or dark coalfish (*Pollachius virens*). See *sej*.

mål measurement or measurements.

måle to measure.

måltid meal or mealtime.

nakkekotelet pork neck chop (not usually available in the US).

natmad midnight snack.

natron washing soda (sodium carbonate decahydrate), also used in baking.

nektarin nectarine.

nelliker cloves.

nescafe instant coffee (like Kleenex, this started out as a brand name). Also called *pulverkaffe*.

nudel noodle. The plural of *nudel* is *nudler*.

nybagt freshly baked.

nyde to enjoy, appreciate.

nye kartofler the first harvested potatoes. These very small potatoes are considered a delicacy when they appear in late May or early June.

nyre kidney.

nød nut. The plural of *nød* is *nødder*.

oksebryst beef brisket.

oksehøjreb prime rib.

oksekød beef.

oksemørbrad beef tenderloin.

olie oil.

oliven olive or olives.

olivenolie olive oil.

opdrættede fisk farmed fish.

opskrift recipe.

orange the color orange. The fruit is *appelsin* in Danish.

ost cheese.

osv abbreviation for *og så videre*, "and so forth," equivalent to etc.

ovn oven.

ovnbagt oven baked.

panderistet pan toasted, pan fried.

paneret breaded.

paradisæbler crab apples.

paranødder Brazil nuts.

parmaskinke Parma ham.

pastille lozenge.

pastinak parsnip.

peber pepper.

peberfrugt bell pepper.

pebermølle peppermill.

peberrod horseradish, often eaten freshly grated (*høvlet peberrod*).

pekannød pecan.

perlehøne guinea fowl.

perleløg pearl onions.

perlesukker coarse granulated sugar crystals.

persille parsley.

persillerod parsley root (*Petroselinum crispum* var. *tuberosum*).

pickles pickles, including the type served on hot dogs.

pighaj spiny dogfish (*Squalus acanthias*).

pighvar turbot (*Psetta maxima*).

pilsner lager beer with strong hops flavor.

pindemad appetizers on toothpicks.

pinjekerner pine nuts.

piskefløde whipping cream.

pisket fløde whipped cream, which is served unsweetened in Denmark. Also called *flødeskum*.

pistachionød pistachio.

porrer leeks.

porsesnaps *snaps* flavored with bog myrtle (*Myrica gale*).

postej pâté, as in *leverpostej* (liver pâté).

potaske potash (a baking ingredient similar to baking soda). Called potassium carbonate in the US and Canada, it is often available in drugstores.

proptrækker corkscrew.

pulver powder, dry mix.

pulverkaffe instant (powdered) coffee. Also called *nescafe*.

purløg chives.

pære pear.

pølser sausages, hot dogs.

pølsevogn hot dog stand.

på on or on top of.

på køl set out on a counter or put in a refrigerator to cool.

pålæg literally "on lay," *pålæg* is a generic term for cold cuts, meat, salad, fish, or cheese used as a topping on *smørrebrød*.

pålægschokolade wafer-thin rectangles of milk or dark chocolate, eaten atop *rugbrød* or *franskbrød*.

påskebryg Easter beer, a strong seasonal beer.

quark soft, creamy low-fat curd cheese used as a baking ingredient or spread. Also spelled *kvark*.

quinoa quinoa.

rabarber rhubarb.

radise radish.

ramsløg type of wild garlic called ramsons (*Allium ursinum*). The leaves are a delicacy available only in the spring.

raps rapeseed.

rapsolie rapeseed oil, canola oil.

rasp bread crumbs.

regnbueis ice cream in a rainbow of flavors.

regnbueørred rainbow trout (*Oncorhynchus mykiss*). Also called *forel*.

regningen the check or bill.

rejer shrimp. See also *fjordrejer*.

remonce Danish pastry filling or topping made from creamed butter and sugar. *Remonce* may be flavored with cinnamon, marzipan, or nuts.

ret course or dish. A *varm ret* is warm or hot; a *koldt ret* is a cold dish.

ribs red currant(s).

ribsgelé red currant jelly.

rimmet describes raw fish or shellfish that has been prepared by layering it in salt, sugar, and pepper for hours.

ris rice.

riste to toast.

ristet brød toasted bread, toast.

ristede løg crispy onions, often served alongside a *rød pølse* (red hot dog).

rod root.

roe rutabaga or Swedish turnip (*Brassica napobrassica*). Also called *kålroe*.

rogn roe (fish eggs) from cod, sturgeon, and other fish.

rom rum.

rosenkål Brussels sprouts.

rosin raisin.

rosmarin rosemary.

rug rye.

rugbrød dense square rye bread, usually sliced thin. *Rugbrød* is sometimes sold in the US as Westphalian pumpernickel, but it is not like other types of American pumpernickel. See page 45 for a recipe.

rugmel rye flour.

rundtenom one slice of *rugbrød*, enough for two half-slice *smørrebrød*.

rygeost smoked curd cheese from Funen (*Fyn*).

rød red.

rødbeder beets, usually served pickled.

rødfisk redfish (*Sebastes marinus*).

rødkål red cabbage, served cooked as a sweet-and-sour side dish or garnish.

rødspætte European plaice (*Pleuronectes platessa*), a flatfish related to flounder.

rødtunge lemon sole (*Microstomus kitt*).

rødvin red wine.

røgeri smokehouse.

røget smoked.

rønnebær rowanberry, mountain ash berry (*Sorbus aucuparia*). Also refers to the plural.

røre stir.

rørsukker cane sugar.

rå raw.

rådyr venison.

råvarer raw materials or ingredients.

safran saffron.

saft concentrated fruit juice.

saftevand juice made from concentrate.

saftig juicy.

Saga mild Danish cheese that is a cross between blue cheese and brie.

salat lettuce; may also mean salad.

salathoved head of lettuce. Also called *hovedsalat*.

salt salt.

saltbøsse salt shaker.

saltet salted.

saltlakrids salty licorice, which contains ammonium chloride. In Denmark it is sometimes called *salmiak lakrids*, which means "ammonia licorice."

salvie sage.

samfundshjælper slang for a beer bottle opener. *Samfundshjælper* literally means "social helper."

Samsø mild, nutty, cow's milk cheese similar to Emmentaler. Named after the island of Samsø. Also spelled Samsoe.

sandart zander or pike-perch (*Stizostedion lucioperca*).

sandwich a sandwich with bread on the top and bottom—not open-faced.

sardin sardine or European pilchard (*Sardina pilchardus*).

sauce gravy, sauce.

sej pollock, saithe, or coalfish. Light coalfish (*Pollachius pollachius*) is also called *lyssej,* and dark coalfish (*Pollachius virens*) is also called *mørksej.*

selleri celery root, celeriac. Also called *knoldselleri. Celery* is *bladselleri.*

sennep mustard.

sennepsmel mustard powder.

serviet napkin.

sesamfrø sesame seeds.

sesamolie sesame oil.

sigte sift.

sigtebrød bread made with a mixture of rye and wheat flours.

sild herring (*Clupea harengus*).

simre simmer.

simreret a dish that is simmered over low heat for a long time.

sirup syrup, usually golden (sugar) syrup.

skal shell or tart shell.

skaldyr shellfish.

skalle common roach fish (*Rutilus rutilus*).

Skalling a prize-winning, firm cow's milk cheese from western Jutland.

skalotteløg shallot.

skank shank.

ske spoon.

skildpadde turtle.

skinke ham.

skive slice (of bacon or cheese, for example).

skiveskåren sliced, cut into slices.

skorpe crust (of bread).

skorper rusks.

skovsvampe wild, or forest, mushrooms.

skrubbe flounder, European flounder (*Platichthys flesus*), similar to *rødspætte*.

skræl peel.

skrællet peeled.

skummetmælk skim milk. Also called *minimælk*. Lowfat milk is *letmælk*.

skvalderkål goutweed or ground elder (*Aegopodium podagraria*). The name of this wild spring leaf vegetable literally means "cackle cabbage." However, it is not a member of the cabbage family.

sky meat jelly.

skyr cultured dairy product from Iceland, similar to strained yogurt.

skysovs meat jelly sauce.

skæreost any cheese firm enough to be sliced.

skærising witch flounder or Torbay sole, a North Atlantic flatfish (*Glyptocephalus cynoglossus*).

skært sliced.

skål bowl. Also means "Cheers!"

slagter butcher.

slethvar brill fish (*Scophthalmus rhombus*).

smag taste (noun).

smage to taste.

smagsprøve a sample or taste.

smelte melt.

smilende æg "smiling" egg, cooked halfway between hard-boiled and soft-boiled. Often halved and used as a garnish.

smør butter.

smørstegt sautéed in butter.

små little or small. When describing a single item the adjective is *lille*.

småkager cookies (in England, biscuits). Literally, "little cakes."

småretter side dishes or appetizers.

snaps strong spirits distilled from potatoes or grains. Also called *akvavit* (and spelled *schnapps* in German). Traditionally served with meals, not as an aperitif.

snegle snails.

snitter literally, "little slices," this term can refer to small *smørrebrød* or pastry bars cut from a pan (see *hindbærsnitter*, *Menu Guide*).

sodavand soda, pop.

soja soy. Also spelled *soya*.

sojabønner soybeans. Also spelled *soyabønner*.

solbær black currant(s).

solsikkefrø sunflower seeds.

sommer summer.

sort black.

sortebær black crowberry (*Empetrum nigrum*). Also refers to the plural.

sovs sauce or gravy.

specialøl specialty beer.

spidskommen cumin.

spidskål oxheart or pointed cabbage (*Brassica oleracea* var. *conica*).

spinat spinach.

spise to eat.

spisebord dining table.

spisekort menu. Also called *menukort*.

spiselig edible.

spiseske tablespoon. Abbreviated *spsk*.

sprængt corned, as in corned beef.

sprød crisp.

spsk. abbreviation for tablespoon (*spiseske*).

sprut slang for alcoholic drinks, booze.

spæk fat, lard.

squash squash or zucchini. Also an orange soft drink made by Carlsberg.

stegt fried.

stempelkaffe *café filtre* (plunger coffee).

stenbider lumpfish, lumpsucker (*Cyclopterus lumpus*).

stenbiderrogn lumpfish caviar or roe.

stenformalet mel stone-ground flour.

stikkelsbær gooseberry or gooseberries.

stor big.

storkenæb flowering herb cranesbill or wild geranium (*Geranium maculatum*). Also called simply *geranium*.

storkøb bulk purchase.

strimler strips. When referring to pickles, *i strimler* means "in spears."

struds ostrich.

stuvet creamed; served in a thick béchamel sauce.

stykke piece.

stødt ground.

stør sturgeon, a fish in the family Acipenseridae.

sukat candied fruit peel, succade.

sukker sugar.

sukkerbrunet caramelized, browned in sugar (usually referring to potatoes).

sulten hungry. *Lækkersulten* means hungry for a snack or something sweet.

supermarked supermarket.

suppe soup.

sur sour.

sur-sød sweet and sour.

surdej sourdough.

surkål sauerkraut.

svamp mushroom.

Svenbo firm, Emmentaler-style cheese made from cow's milk.

sveske prune.

svin pig.

svinekam pork neck.

svinekoteletter pork chops.

svinekød pork.

svinemørbrad pork tenderloin. Also called simply *mørbrad*.

svær pork rind crackling. Also called *flæskesvær*.

sydesalt special "simmered" sea salt from Northern Jutland.

syltet pickled.

syltetøj jam.

syrnet fløde sour cream, similar to crème fraîche but with a very low percentage of fat.

særlig special.

sæson season.

sød sweet.

sødkartoffel sweet potato. Also called *batat*.

sødmælk whole milk, 3.5 percent fat. The name literally means "sweet milk."

sølvbede silver beet foliage, a type of chard. Also known as *husmandsasparges*, "poor man's asparagus," because its flavor is similar to asparagus.

søtunge common sole, Dover sole (*solea solea*). Also called simply *tunge*, which can mean tongue (as in calf's tongue).

tallerken plate.

tallerkensmækker nasturtium (*Tropaeolum majus*). Also called *nasturtium*. The leaves and flowers are edible, and the seeds can be used in place of capers. The name *tallerkensmækker* literally means "plate smasher."

tandstik toothpick.

tang seaweed.

tavleretter today's specials (written on a blackboard).

te tea.

teske teaspoon. Abbreviated *tsk*.

tigerrejer tiger prawns or shrimp.

tilbehør accompanying side dishes, garnishes.

time hour.

timian thyme.

tomat tomato.

tomatsovs tomato sauce.

toppet med topped with.

torsk cod, Atlantic cod (*Gadus morhua*).

torskefilet fillet of cod.

torskerogn cod roe. Can be purchased canned, fresh "in a pair of pants," or cooked (*kogt torskerogn*).

tournedos tournedos, small, round slices from the end of a beef tenderloin.

tranebær small cranberry or cranberries (*Vaccinium oxycoccos*).

trekornsblanding a blend of three grains: rye flour, wheat or flaxseed, and sunflower seeds.

trifli trifle.

trimmet cut into a certain shape. Another word for *trimmet* is *udskåret*.

trøffel truffle, the mushroom. May, also refer to a chocolate truffle.

tsk. abbreviation for teaspoon (*teske*).

tun tuna fish. Also called *tunfisk*.

tunge cow's or calf's tongue, served corned. See also the fish *søtunge,* which is also called simply *tunge*.

Tybo mild, cream-colored cow's milk cheese similar to Samsø.

tykmælk popular dairy product similar to a mild form of yogurt. It can be made at home from whole, unpasteurized milk.

tyttebær lingonberry or cowberry (*Vaccinium vitis-idaea*). Refers to both the singular and plural.

tært tart or pie.

tøndemodnet aged in a barrel.

tør dry. *Tørrede* means dried, as in *tørrede abrikoser* (dried apricots).

tørstig thirsty.

udbenet boneless.

uden without.

uden brus non-carbonated.

udsalg on sale at a discounted price.

udskåret cut into a certain shape. Another word for *udskåret* is *trimmet*.

udtræk extract.

udvalg choice, selection.

udvandet diluted.

umoden unripe.

urt herb.

urtete herbal tea.

vaffel waffle. In Denmark waffles are sometimes heart shaped. The plural of *vaffel* is *vafler*. See also *franske vafler* in the *Menu Guide*.

vagtel quail.

valnød walnut.

vand water.

vandmelon watermelon.

vanille vanilla. Also spelled *vanilje*.

vanillesukker sugar that has been flavored with vanilla.

varm chokolade hot chocolate.

varme drikke hot drinks.

varm warm or hot.

vegetar vegetarian.

verdens bedste "world's best."

vild wild.

vildt wild game.

vin wine.

vinblad grape leaf (literally, "wine leaf").

vindruekerneolie grapeseed oil.

vindruer grapes. Also called simply *druer*.

vineddike wine vinegar.

vinmenu wine menu.

vinrabarber rhubarb with thin red stems.

vinstue wine bar.

vinter winter.

vægt weight.

vælge to choose or select.

vælling gruel.

ylette light yogurt.

ymer a type of yogurt.

ymerdrys bread crumbs from rye bread (*rugbrød*) mixed with sugar; used as topping for *ymer* and other yogurt products.

yoghurt yogurt.

zittauerløg giant zittau onion, a yellow heirloom varietal.

zucchini zucchini, green squash.

æble apple.

æbleeddike cider vinegar (literally, "apple vinegar"). Another word for cider vinegar is *cidereddike*.

æblemos apple purée, applesauce.

æblemost apple cider (non-alcoholic).

æg egg, eggs.

æggeblomme egg yolk.

æggehvide egg white.

ælte to knead.

ænder ducks. The singular of *ænder* is *and*.

ærter peas.

økologisk organic. Also called simply *øko*.

øl beer.

øloplukker beer bottle opener.

ørred trout. See also *havørred* and *lakseørred*.

øster oyster.

østershat oyster mushroom.

ål eel, European eel (*Anguilla anguilla*).

årstider seasons.

Food Establishments

A Quick Reference Guide to Restaurants Visited

Research for this book involved visiting many food establishments in Denmark and even one in New York. The chefs and authors we worked with are listed in the *Acknowledgements* (p. xi), and some of their recipes appear in *Tastes of Denmark* (p. 43).

If you wish to contact a restaurant for a reservation or information, it is probably easiest to do it via e-mail. However if you decide to phone from the U.S., you must first dial 011 for an international call, and then use the country code for Denmark, which is 45. (Calls within Denmark do not require either of these.)

Restaurants

Aamanns Øster Farimagsgade   12, 2100 Copenhagen Ø
 Tel (45) 35 55 33 10   www.aamanns.dk
 info@aamanns.dk
Brdr. Price i Tivoli   Tivoli, Vesterbrogade 3, 1630 Copenhagen V
 Tel (45) 38 41 51 51   http://tivoli.brdr-price.dk
 info.tivoli@brdr-price.dk
Conditori La Glace   Skoubogade 3, 1158 Copenhagen K
 Tel (45) 33 14 46 46   www.laglace.dk
 conditori@laglace.dk
The Copenhagen   13 Laight St, New York, NY 10013
 Tel 212-925-1313   www.thecopenhagennyc.com
 info@thecopenhagennyc.com
Den Gamle By   Viborgvej 2, 8000 Århus C
 Tel (45) 86 12 31 88   www.dengamleby.dk
 mail@dengamleby.dk

Den Røde Cottage   Strandvejen 550, 2930 Klampenborg
Tel (45) 39 90 46 14   www.dengulecottage.dk
info@dengulecottage.dk

Den Skaldede Kok, Tivoli   Chef Carsten Olsen has closed his restaurant and
is now running his own catering company in Helsingør.

Hotel Orø Kro   Bygaden 57, Øro, 4300 Holbæk
Tel (45) 59 47 00 06   www.oroekro.dk
reception@oroekro.dk

Malling & Schmidt og Kähler Design Villa Dining   Chef Torsten Schmidt
closed the restaurant we visited (Malling & Schmidt), and re-opened it as
this establishment.
Grenåvej 127, 8240 Risskov (Århus)
Tel (45) 86 17 70 88   www.villadining.dk
info@villadining.dk

Marv & Ben   Snaregade 4, 1205 Copenhagen K
Tel (45) 33 91 01 91   www.cargocollective.com/marvogben
reservation@marvogben.dk

Norsminde Kro   Gl. Krovej 2, 8300 Odder
Tel (45) 86 93 24 44   www.norsminde-kro.dk
norsminde@norsminde-kro.dk

Restaurant Carlslund   Fruens Bøge Skov 7, 5250 Odense SV
Tel (45) 65 91 11 25   www.restaurant-carlslund.dk
kontakt@restaurant-carlslund.dk

Restaurant Els   Store Strandestræde 3, 1255 Copenhagen K
Tel (45) 33 14 13 41   www.restaurant-els.dk
els@restaurant-els.dk

Restaurant Gammel Mønt   Gammel Mønt 41, 1117 Copenhagen K
Tel (45) 33 15 10 60   www.gammel-moent.dk

Restaurant Grøften, Tivoli   Vesterbrogade 3, 1620 Copenhagen V
Tel (45) 33 75 06 75   www.groeften.dk
info@groeften.dk

Sortebro Kro   Sejerskovvej 20, 5260 Odense S
Tel (45) 66 13 28 26   www.sortebrokro.dk
smag@sortebro.dk

Søstrene Olsen   Øresundsvej 10, 3100 Hornbæk
Tel (45) 49 70 05 50   www.sostreneolsen.dk
restaurant@sostreneolsen.dk

Bibliography

Andersen, Lynn. *Modern Danish Cooking*. Copenhagen: Nyt Nordisk Forlag Arnold Busck, 2014.

Christensen, Bent. *New Nordic Cuisine: Interpretations of 16 of Denmark's Best Restaurants*. Danish/English text. Copenhagen: Politikens Forlag, 2012.

Crafts, Kevin. *Ebelskivers: Filled Pancakes and Other Mouthwatering Miniatures*. San Francisco: Weldon Owen, 2010.

Davidsen, Ida. *Open Your Heart to the Danish Open [Sandwich]... The Davidsen Dynasty and Their Best Recipes*, 2nd ed. Copenhagen: Lindhardt & Ringhof, 2004.

Dern, Judith H. *Danish Food & Cooking*. London: Aquamarine/Anness Publishing, 2008 and 2001.

Diehl, Kari Schoening. *The Everything Nordic Cookbook*. Avon, MA: Adams Media, 2012.

Gold, Carol. *Danish Cookbooks: Domesticity & National Identity, 1616–1901*. Seattle: University of Washington Press, 2007.

Hahnemann, Tina. *The Nordic Diet: Using Local and Organic Food to Promote a Healthy Lifestyle*. New York: Skyhorse Publishing, 2011.

Hahnemann, Tina. *Scandinavian Christmas*. New York: Sterling, 2013.

Hahnemann, Tina. *The Scandinavian Cookbook*. New York: Andrews McMeel Publishing, 2009.

Hansen, Stig. *Cooking Danish: A Taste of Denmark*. Nashville: Favorite Recipes Press, 2007.

Jensen, Birthe Karen. *Sweet on Denmark: Contemporary Danish Desserts*. Mulgrave, Australia: The Images Publishing Group, 2011.

Johansen, Signe. *Scandilicious: Secrets of Scandinavian Cooking*. London: Hodder & Stoughton, 2011.

Klinken, Katrine. *Smørrebrød: Danish Open*. Copenhagen: Narayana Press, 2008.

Kolos, Marianne Stagetorn. *Fairy Tale Cakes from La Glace*. Adapted from Hans Christian Andersen. Copenhagen: PP Forlag, 2004.

Larson, Kirsten. *Only One Slice: Danish Sandwiches/Smørrebrød*. Privately published, 1998.

McDonald, Julie Jensen. *Danish Touches: Recipes and Reflections*, 2nd ed. (a revision and compilation of *Delectably Danish: Recipes and Reflections* and *Definitely Danish*). Iowa City: Penfield Books, 2013.

Meyer, Arthur L. *Danish Cooking and Baking Traditions*. New York: Hippocrene Books, 2011.

Mink, Miisa. *Nordic Bakery Cookbook*. New York: Ryland, Peters & Small, 2011.

Moran, Rachel and Emma Sørgaard. *Philosophical Food Crumbs: A Kierkegaard Cookbook*. CreateSpace Independent Publishing Platform, 2013.

Mosesson, Anne, Janet Laurence, and Judith H. Dern. *The Food and Cooking of Scandinavia: Sweden, Norway, Denmark*. London: Lorenz/Anness Publishing, 2011.

Plum, Camilla. *The Scandinavian Kitchen: Over 100 Essential Ingredients with 200 Authentic Recipes*. London: Kyle Books, 2011.

Redzepi, René. *Noma: Time and Place in Nordic Cuisine*. London: Phaidon Press, 2010.

Riggs, Lisa Steen. *Æbleskiver and More: A Sampling of Danish Recipes*. Iowa City: Penfield Books, 2003.

Saulsbury, Camilla. *150 Best Ebelskiver Recipes*. Toronto: Robert Rose, 2013.

Serra, Daniel and Hanna Tunberg. *An Early Meal: A Viking Age Cookbook & Culinary Odyssey*. Furulund, Sweden: ChronoCopia Publishing, 2013

The Cookbook Committee of the Danish Lutheran Churches in British Columbia. *Best of Danish Heritage Cookbook and More*. Burnaby, Canada: The Danish Lutheran Church of Vancouver, undated.

Troelsø, Ole. *Insider's Guide to Smørrebrød*. Amazon Digital Services, 2013. In Danish, *Smørrebrød i Danmark*. Copenhagen: Forlaget Lucullus, 2013.

Yen, Dagmarette. *Glædelig Jul: A Danish Christmas Recipe Book*. CreateSpace Independent Publishing Platform, 2010.

Online references

- The official Web site of Denmark: www.denmark.dk
- Danish culture and customs: www.danishnet.com
- Danish news in English: http://politiken.dk/newsinenglish and www.cphpost.dk
- A film-focused look at the Danish experience in America: http://danes.tv
- Danish culture blog from US: www.wonderful-denmark.com
- Regulations regarding taking food from Denmark to the U.S. (*leverpostej*, *spegepølse*, and *rullepølse* are not allowed, for example): http://denmark.usembassy.gov
- Christian's Danish Recipes blog: www.mindspring.com/~cborgnaes
- *Smørrebrød* blog from Canada: www.danishsandwich.com
- New Scandinavian Cooking (a few recipes from Denmark): www.newscancook.com
- DR Television Food Shows (in Danish): www.dr.dk/Mad
- Danish to English translation app: www.gramtrans.com

Index

allspice *allehånde* 107
almond *mandel* 30–31, 36, 38, 89, 95,
   97–103, 105, 122
anchovy *ansjos* 108
anise *anis* 96, 108
appetizers *appetitvækker* 40–42,
   85–86, 108, 113, 125, 129
apple *æble* 4–5, 9, 24, 28–30, 37, 85,
   89, 93, 100, 102–104, 106,
   108, 110, 122, 134
   cider *æblemost* 134
   sauce *æblemos* 134
apricot *abrikos* 102, 107, 132
aquavit *akvavit (snaps)* 5, 9, 31–33,
   35–36, 41, 85, 95, 103,
   106–108, 110, 114, 116, 120,
   125, 129
artichoke *artiskok* 108, 118
asparagus *asparges* 24, 41, 94–95,
   105, 108, 116, 131

banana *banan* 108
barley *byg* 4–7, 31–32, 88–89, 102,
   105, 110
basil *basilikum* 108
bay leaf *laurærblad* 121
bean *bønne* 4–5, 110, 115–116, 119, 130
   bean sprout *bønne spire* 110
beef *oksekød* 14, 19, 22–23, 32, 35,
   42, 88–90, 92–93, 95, 98–99,
   101–103, 105, 108, 115, 124,
   130, 132

beer *øl* 5–7, 12, 14, 16, 29, 35–36,
   40–41, 45, 85–86, 106, 112–
   113, 117–118, 122, 125–126,
   128, 130, 134
beet *rødbede* 19, 24, 85, 88–90, 93,
   96, 99, 104, 116, 127, 131
bell pepper *peberfrugt* 125
berry *bær* 4, 17, 24, 32–33, 35, 85,
   98, 101, 104, 110, 112, 115,
   120, 127, 130
blackberry *brombær* 109
blueberry *blåbær* 109
bok choy *kinakål* 119
boysenberry *boysenbær* 109
bread *brød* 4–7, 9, 11–12, 14, 19–24,
   26, 28–32, 36, 40–41, 83–85,
   87, 89–95, 97–98, 100–106,
   108, 110, 113–114, 119,
   126–129, 134
bream *brazen* 109
broccoli *brokkoli* 109
Brussels sprouts *rosenkål* 127
buckwheat *boghvede* 29, 109

cabbage *kål* 8, 19–20, 24, 26–27,
   31, 36–38, 40, 85, 88–89, 91,
   97–98, 101–102, 104, 112,
   116, 119, 127, 129–130
cabbage turnip *knudekål* 119
cake *kage* 12, 24–32, 39, 42,
   88–92, 95–99, 101–106, 118,
   120–121, 129

candy *guf* 25–26, 30, 36, 39, 42, 89, 94, 96, 99, 109, 114–115, 118, 120
capers *kapers* 22, 90, 95, 97, 99–100, 118, 131
caramel (toffee) *flødekaramel* 113, 118
caraway *kommen* 9, 29, 33, 35, 101, 111, 120
cardamom *kardemomme* 36, 89, 94–95, 105, 118
carp *karpefisk* 119
carrot *gulerod* 5, 8, 24, 29, 88, 94–95, 98–99, 105, 115
cashew *cashewnød* 110
catfish *havkat* 115, 120
cauliflower *blomkål* 109
celeriac *knoldselleri* 119, 128
celery *bladselleri* 109, 119, 128
cheese *ost* 1, 4–5, 11–12, 16, 22, 27–29, 35, 83–84, 87, 92, 96, 99, 102, 109, 111–115, 117, 120, 122–124, 126–129, 131–132
cherry *kirsebær* 25, 29, 38, 90, 96, 100, 110, 119, 123
chervil *kørvel* 121
chestnut *kastanje* 119
chicken *kylling* 5, 23, 41, 85, 92–94, 97–98, 100, 104–105, 115, 117, 121
chickpeas *kikærter* 119
chive *purløg* 20, 35, 89, 96, 102–103, 126
chocolate *chokolade* 12, 20, 24–25, 28, 30, 35, 40–41, 85–86, 89–91, 94–103, 105, 107, 110, 118, 120, 126, 132–133
cider *most* 123
cinnamon *kanel* 36–37, 89, 95–96, 100, 104, 118, 126
cloudberry *multebær* 123
cloves *nelliker* 89, 124
coalfish *sej* 121, 124, 128
coconut *kokos* 90–91, 98, 119–120, 122

cod *torsk* 5, 7, 23–24, 34, 39, 88, 95–96, 99, 104, 109, 119, 121, 127, 132
coffee *kaffe* 9, 12, 26–27, 29, 31–32, 40, 42, 83–86, 90, 95, 107, 112, 118, 123–125, 130
cold cuts *pålæg* 29, 126
cookies *småkager* 4, 13, 24–27, 30–31, 36, 88–89, 91–99, 101, 103, 105, 112–113, 119, 129
coriander *koriander* 120
corn *majs* 112, 120, 122
crab *krabbe* 120, 125
crayfish *krebs* 120–121
cream *fløde* 4, 9, 14, 24–25, 28–31, 35, 37–38, 40, 42, 85, 87–103, 105–106, 110–111, 113, 115, 117, 120, 125–126, 131–132
cucumber *agurk* 19–20, 22, 24, 85, 88, 92, 103, 107–108
cumin *spidskommen* 29, 120, 130
custard *kagecreme* 12, 28, 67, 102, 111, 118
cuttlefish *blæksprutte* 109

dessert *dessert* 9, 24, 20, 32, 36–39, 42, 83, 85, 88, 90–93, 95–97, 99–100, 106, 111
dill *dild* 9, 27, 33, 90, 93, 95, 102, 111, 120
drink *drik* 5, 9, 24, 32, 42, 83, 86, 111, 123, 129–130, 134
duck *and* 37, 41–42, 88–89, 101, 103, 107–108, 134

eel *ål* 23, 35, 102, 104, 134
egg *æg* 23, 25, 30–32, 35, 40–41, 84–85, 88–92, 96, 99–100, 102–106, 117, 122, 129, 134
eggplant *aubergine* 108
elderberry *hyldebær* 24, 117
European plaice *rødspætte* 23, 84, 99, 101, 104–105, 127

fennel *fennikel* 112

fish *fisk* 1–2, 5, 7–8, 11, 16–17, 22–23, 27, 32–35, 41, 85, 87–88, 91–92, 96, 98, 101, 105, 107–109, 112–113, 115, 117, 119, 121, 124, 126–130, 132

flaxseed *hørfrø* 117, 132

flounder *skrubbe* 127, 129

fruit *frugt* 1, 4, 16–17, 24, 29, 35, 84, 86–88, 91–92, 95, 97–98, 101, 104, 108, 110, 114–115, 120, 124, 127, 131

game *dyrevildt* 2, 5, 17, 111, 133

garfish *hornfisk* 23, 116

garlic *hvidløg* 41, 109, 117, 126

gelatin *husblas* 104, 116

ginger *ingefær* 117

goat *ged* 5, 114

goose *gås* 37, 41–42, 89, 93, 101, 104, 115

grape *vindrue* 111, 133

grapefruit *grapefrugt* 114

gurnard *knurhane* 119

haddock *kuller* 120

hake *kulmule* 120

halibut *helleflynder* 94, 101, 116

ham *skinke* 31, 38, 84, 88, 93–94, 97–99, 102, 105, 125, 128

hare *hare* 92, 115

hazelnut *hasselnød* 31, 115

heart *hjerte* 31, 91, 94, 116, 133

herbs *krydderurter* 33, 81, 114, 120, 122, 130, 133

herring *sild* 5, 7, 19, 23–24, 28, 34–35, 84, 88, 95–98, 102–105, 128

honey *honning* 5, 31, 35, 94, 99, 116, 123

horseradish *peberrod* 19, 85, 90, 95, 99–100, 105, 125

hot dogs *pølser* 20–22, 88, 92, 94, 100–101, 104, 106, 125–126

ice cream *flødeis* (*is*) 24–25, 35, 42, 85, 91–92, 100–101, 103, 110, 113, 115, 117, 120, 126

icing *glasur* 40, 42, 90, 94, 97–98, 114

jam *syltetøj* 12, 24–25, 31–32, 35, 37, 42, 83, 88, 91, 93, 96–97, 99, 101–103, 106, 122, 131

jelly *gelé* 15, 24, 88, 90, 92–93, 98, 101, 114, 126, 129

juice *juice* 28, 86, 90, 108, 118, 127

kale *grønkål* 8, 24, 31, 38–39, 93–94, 97, 115, 119

kidney *nyre* 91, 119, 124

kohlrabi *knudekål* 119, 121

lamb *lam* 29, 32, 41, 95, 100–101, 109, 121

leeks *porrer* 95, 125

legumes *bælgfrugter* 110

lemon *citron* 19–20, 85, 90, 96, 102–104, 110, 127

lentils *linser* 121

lettuce *salat* 24, 116, 118, 127

licorice *lakrids* 24–26, 35, 71–72, 103, 121, 128

lingonberry *tyttebær* 132

liqueur *likør* 25, 86, 93, 110, 121

liver *lever* 15, 19, 90–91, 93, 95, 97, 121, 125

lobster *hummer* 33, 116, 118, 121

lumpfish *stenbider* 104

mackerel *makrel* 98, 122

marjoram *merian* 123

marzipan *marcipan* 12, 25, 30, 38–39, 42, 89, 91, 93, 95–96, 98, 105, 122, 126

meat *kød* 1, 4–8, 11, 14, 19, 21–22, 29, 32, 34, 38, 40–41, 84–85, 87–90, 93, 96–104, 108, 121, 126, 129

melon *melon* 116, 123
milk *mælk* 4–5, 7, 14–15, 20, 22,
    28–29, 35, 37, 83, 85, 89, 91,
    95–98, 100, 103, 106–107,
    111–112, 114–115, 118, 121–123,
    126, 128–129, 131–132
millet *hirse* 116
mint *mynte* 123
molasses *melasse* 123
mousse *fromage* 42, 85, 90, 98, 113
mushroom *svamp* 4, 110, 118–119,
    131–132, 134
mussels *muslinger* 2, 33, 109, 123
mustard *sennep* 21–22, 32, 35, 39–40,
    93, 96, 99–102, 104, 128

nectarine *nektarin* 124
needlefish *hornfisk* 116
noodle *nudel* 124
nut *nød* 4, 17, 98–99, 106, 124–126
nutmeg *muskat* 123

oats *havregryn* 4, 6, 115
octopus *blæksprutte* 109
olive *oliven* 124
onion *løg* 4, 19–20, 22–23, 29,
    85, 88–93, 96, 98–99, 102,
    104–106, 113, 122, 125–126,
    134
orange *appelsin* 39, 93, 108–109, 124,
    130
    juice *appelsinjuice* 108
ostrich *struds* 130
oyster *øster* 2, 33, 119, 134

parsley *persille* 9, 22, 88, 92, 94–95,
    100–101, 103–104, 109, 120,
    125
parsley root *persillerod* 125
parsnip *pastinak* 125
pâté *postej* 15, 19, 90, 93, 95–97, 125
peas *ærter* 5, 29, 87–88, 93–95, 98,
    104–105, 113, 115, 134

peach *fersken* 104, 112
peanut *jordnød* 15, 118
pear *pære* 5, 28, 100, 126
pecan *pikannød* 125
pepper *peber* 89, 92, 100–101, 125–126
    chile pepper *chilipeber* 110
perch *aborre* 107
pheasant *fasan* 112
pickles *pickles* 22, 99–100, 108, 125,
    130
pike-perch *sandart* 128
pineapple *ananas* 107
pine nuts *pinjekerner* 125
pistachio *pistachionød* 125
plum *blomme* 29, 89, 104, 109, 123
pollock *lyssej* 121, 124, 128
pomegranate *granatæble* 114
pork *svinekød* 5, 7–9, 14–15, 17,
    19–20, 22–24, 29–32,
    35–38, 40, 42, 87–89, 91–98,
    100–106, 112–114, 124, 131
porridge *grød* 4–5, 7, 14, 37, 85, 89,
    93–94, 96, 100, 105–106, 115
potato *kartoffel* 1, 9, 11, 17, 19–20,
    22–24, 29, 32–33, 36–38, 41,
    85, 88–96, 98–100, 102–105,
    108, 113, 119, 124, 129, 131
poultry *fjerkræ* 35, 37, 87, 112
prune *sveske* 31, 93, 103–105, 131
pudding *budding* 32, 38, 85, 93, 96,
    100–102, 106, 110, 115
pumpkin *græskar* 115

quail *vagtel* 133
quince *kvæde* 120

rabbit *kanin* 118
radish *radise* 20, 24, 29, 103, 126
raisin *rosin* 31, 101, 105, 127
raspberry *hindbær* 24, 88, 94, 99,
    106, 116
rhubarb *rabarber* 24–25, 41, 85, 93,
    100, 126, 133

rice *ris* 24, 37–38, 89, 96, 98,
100–101, 109, 115, 126
roe *rogn* 2, 85, 104, 121, 127, 130, 132
rowanberry *rønnebær* 127
rusks *skorper* 105, 129
rutabaga *roe* 121, 127
rye *rug* 4–7, 19, 24, 31, 35, 83, 87–88,
90, 101, 110, 127–128, 132,
134

saffron *safran* 36, 127
saithe *sej* 121, 124, 128
salad *salat* 20, 22, 24, 29–30, 85, 88,
92, 94, 96, 100, 102, 106–107,
111–112, 126–127
salmon *laks* 7, 23, 34, 84–85, 90,
93–97, 101, 105, 121
sauce (gravy) *sauce* 9, 19, 21–24,
32, 37–40, 87–96, 98–105,
114–115, 120, 122, 128–130,
132
sauerkraut *surkål* 131
sausage *pølser* 5, 7, 20–22, 29, 31, 38,
41, 83–85, 88, 90, 93, 97–98,
100, 103–104
scallops *kammuslinger* 118
seabass *havaborre* 115
seabream *havbras* 115
shallot *skalotteløg* 102, 128
shellfish *skaldyr* 2, 5, 126, 128
shrimp *rejer* 19, 23, 84–85, 100, 102,
104–105, 113, 126, 132
snails *snegle* 129
soda (pop) *sodavand* 86, 129
sole *søtunge* 34, 127, 129, 131
soup *suppe* 29, 31, 40, 42, 85, 87,
91–99, 103–105, 111, 115,
119, 131
soy *soja* 129
spices *krydderi* 9, 15, 31, 81, 89,
91, 93, 96, 100–101, 104,
107–108, 120, 122
spinach *spinat* 108, 130

squash *squash* 115, 130, 134
squid *blæksprutte* 109
strawberry *jordbær* 24–25, 29, 95, 118
sturgeon *stør* 127, 130
sweet potato *batat* 108, 131
syrup *sirup* 32, 64, 89, 100, 107, 128

tarragon *estragon* 112
tart (pie) *tært* 32, 90–91, 95, 97–98,
106, 121, 128, 132
tea *te* 83, 105, 117–118, 133
thyme *timian* 132
tomato *tomat* 24, 91, 93, 98,
105–106, 132
tongue *tunge* 131–132
trout *ørred* 23, 110, 113, 116, 119,
121, 126, 134
tuna *tun* 132
turbot *pighvar* 116, 125
turkey *kalkun* 118
turmeric *gurkemeje* 115
turnip *majroe* 5, 119, 121–122, 127

veal *kalv* 8, 22, 29, 88, 91–92, 95, 97,
101, 104, 109, 118
vegetables *grønsager* 1, 5, 8, 16–17,
24, 27, 29, 38, 40, 84–85, 87,
93–94, 103–104, 112, 115,
122, 129
venison *rådyr* 5, 90, 97, 111, 116, 127

waffle *vaffel* 9, 92, 133
walnut *valnød* 133
watermelon *vandmelon* 133
whale *hval* 116
wheat *hvede* 4–6, 29, 41, 94, 98, 116,
118, 128, 132
whiting *hvilling* 117
wine *vin* 11, 16, 31, 33, 36, 42, 86,
89, 93, 105, 116–117, 122,
127, 133

zucchini *zucchini* 111, 130, 134

design Ekeby
cover design Susan P. Chwae
color printing Traver Graphics, Inc.
book production Sheridan Books, Inc.

typefaces Garamond Simoncini and Helvetica Black
paper 60# House White